Entrepreneur Thinking

(Special Edition 2022)

By Paul Clargo

The Theory of Entrepreneur Thinking

Entrepreneurs are neither Born nor made

ALL People have Entrepreneur Value

Latent Value, Potential Value

Entrepreneur, Intrapreneur and Organisational Value

And our entrepreneur value increases and decreases

As business landscapes evolve in static and chaotic environments

Through managing entrepreneur value

And developing Entrepreneur Thinking In our people

We increase organisational value

And become more competent to recognise opportunity

And deliver, Inimitable competitive advantage!

Entrepreneur Spirit

I remembered watching a TV programme about entrepreneurship. Lord Bilimoria (Cobra Beer) is talking with Peter Jones (Dragon's Den) about what entrepreneurs do:

Lord Bilimoria said,

'Entrepreneurs have an idea,
They want to take it somewhere and
Against all the odds making it happen!'

That's entrepreneurship.

Entrepreneur Thinking

Entrepreneur Thinking, manage themselves and their people to maximise the capture of ideas, the development of exploitable solutions, the achievement of results and the protection of venture rewards that are both tangible and intangible.

That's Entrepreneur Thinking!

Entrepreneur Thinking 2022 Copyright 2022

ISBN: 9781687140791

Imprint: Independently published

Entrepreneur Thinking Copyright © 2022

Entrepreneur Thinking Copyright © 2022© by Paul Clargo

About Entrepreneur Thinking

'Entrepreneur Thinking' focuses on building entrepreneur skills and using these skills to provide benefits for employees. We are developing entrepreneurs for the benefit of employees and their employers. These entrepreneurs within organisations are called 'Intrapreneurs'.

So, rather than following traditional approaches that ask who an entrepreneur is, we are identifying entrepreneur skills and processes and using this knowledge to enhance the skills of our people and the organisation's internal processes. The content has been developed using a four-pronged multi-disciplinary approach (Criminology & Psychology, Economics, Business Leadership & management in theory, and 'What CEO's Want' in practice) - for two main purposes:

1. To develop people, intrapreneurs, entrepreneurs and an entrepreneur culture, in new and mature businesses.
2. To assist the leadership and management and leverage of hidden assets that provides exponential growth and competitive advantage.

'Entrepreneur Thinking is built on the ethos that everyone has the potential to apply their entrepreneur thinking toward a greater goal that may seem untenable as an individual employee but may be more easily realised as part of an organisational team. People have ideas, organisations are looking for growth and can invest in new ideas, technologies, and the necessary infrastructure to support the idea, its development and success (or failure). There is no risk to the employee. The benefits include a culture of entrepreneurship that stimulates creativity, increases the value of individuals, our teams and safeguards employment for the organisation that stimulates local economic activity as well.

People may never raise the investment required to realise an entrepreneurial dream however, with entrepreneur cultures the organisation may help relevant industry ideas to flourish but above all employees will have an opportunity to piece together how entrepreneurs develop and drive businesses to become successful economic powerhouses.

Capital Thinking, Capital is a Value Measure

Capital for most people means investment or money or cash. For us, when we see capital, it means this can be measured. So financial capital is measurable as we just count the £'s or $'s. Measuring people, ideas, processes, relations, and goodwill are more difficult.

With this capital philosophy of Entrepreneur Thinking, all people have entrepreneur capital or the possibility of being entrepreneurial. We are born with zero entrepreneur capital, we build entrepreneur capital as we have life or business experiences, through vocation and education, and our entrepreneur capital eventually wanes and dies. We understand people and entrepreneurs face constraints meaning we may or may not choose to be an intrapreneur or entrepreneurial and start businesses.

For Entrepreneurs who take the entrepreneur leap, they also face internal and external rivalry and fierce competition and demands for liabilities, taxes and lawsuits. Being an entrepreneur is really entering the dragon's den and is the scarier option. However, an intrapreneur's option is a safer route to realise an idea, gain skills, recognition, and satisfaction.

Once we accept that we can build capital both tangible and intangible then we are able to make a difference and grow capital.

How we do this

'Entrepreneur Thinking' is focused on discovering the secrets of entrepreneur skills and developing tools to deliver exponential growth. 'Entrepreneur Thinking' uses academic research, business philosophy and practical application that helps understand entrepreneur thinking as follows:

1. Identify entrepreneur types and roles
2. What do entrepreneurs do? They Organise, Discover, Achieve and Protect
3. Entrepreneur Action Model – How it all fits together
4. The Entrepreneur Driver
5. How you can build entrepreneur capital too!

To do this, research was both broad and deep. Examining entrepreneurs, entrepreneurship, innovation, leadership, and management as well as business experience, entrepreneurs and their mentors. Further, the subject was found to be so important to human behaviour that research must also rely on a multi-discipline approach. This meant a more encompassing approach to include psychology, psychiatry, criminology, sociology as well as economic theory and intellectual capital accounting.

The economic activity of communities to nations is reliant on entrepreneurs and has a duty to understand how enterprise may be increased and improved and how the likelihood of venture survival is supported. While entrepreneurs largely make their own way through the many obstacles to enterprise, developing intrapreneurs is an organisational choice to encourage and educate the workforce about innovation and intrapreneur opportunity, the leadership qualities of entrepreneurs and entrepreneur teams and the entrepreneurs value management control and risk foresight. A Big Challenge!

However, everything can be improved when we have a method of measurement, a simple reliable system that improves the possibility and success of entrepreneurs that anyone can adopt. 'Entrepreneur Thinking will demonstrate how to measure and improve anything. Those non-financial indicators can have a numerical value easily. Then when we can measure it, we can manage it and develop it!

The Problem

If only entrepreneurship was a product or service!
How would an entrepreneur achieve leverage?

Paul Clargo

Keep it Simple Start-up - A third dimension

I only set out to understand why my colleagues valued my opinion on matters above their own! Why didn't these well trained professional people make choices that would make their own roles easier and drive organisational success, they were often much more capable of doing this than me!

Through my research I found there are 2 types of entrepreneurs, 4 roles and 4 main tasks and have been told by entrepreneurs that, if you want it enough you will find a way to achieve it. We want to find a way to help entrepreneurs and to do this we are looking for the ingredients of entrepreneurship and how we can influence the growth of entrepreneurs. So, I developed the third dimension.

What's the third dimension? Simple, it's a scale of entrepreneur personality, business experience, life experience and events and how we apply meaning to these happenings. The foundation is that we are born with zero ability to do anything, as we journey through life, we experience all kinds of situational events that happen externally and are interpreted internally. We give meaning to things based on nurture, nature, family, teachers, friends, the media, our education, religion, and culture and so on. These experiences translated to a business context develops our entrepreneur capabilities, whether that's being creative, finding ways to motivate or to protect life's rewards such as our cash or family relationships, all our experiences can relate to a business relationship if we want them to. At some point our knowledge, skills and experience may converge to a point and 'on comes the light' an idea is born and for whatever reason an entrepreneur is born. How does this happen and is there anything we can do to influence or control the birth or making of entrepreneurs? Can we increase the speed of entrepreneur learning and experience in some way? Arguably, developing entrepreneurs will improve economic activity that will provide many social benefits such as much-needed products and services and jobs.

Thus, if I can show you a proven way to cut the time of your entrepreneur journey and save and make money you'd be interested, wouldn't you? I looked at entrepreneurship with an open mind, beyond the personality traits and beyond successful entrepreneurs (as this is where most research seems to concentrate). I have taken academic studies and evidence about entrepreneurs and entrepreneurship and found a way to transfer the information into knowledge that we can use in a practical way, making sense of knowledge through insight to reach innovative application. Does this sound familiar? Isn't this exactly what entrepreneur's do? This means we can take any subject and identify the key components and measure and improve our performance, even entrepreneurship. Radical thinking but what would this mean to economic activity if we really can do this?

The Secrets of Entrepreneur Thinking

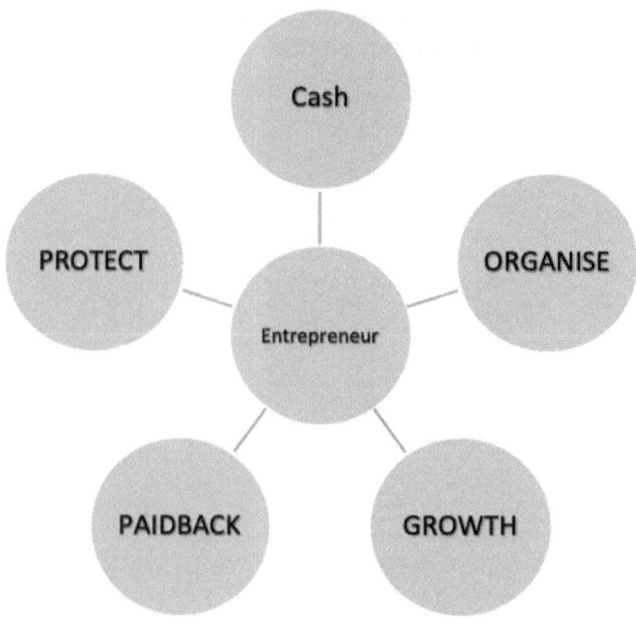

Contents

The Four Entrepreneur Secrets

ORGANISE - Coordinator, Identify Value

Opportunity Recognition
Resources
Growth
Achievement
Niche or Not
Improvise
Stress-tolerance
Exploitation

GROWTH - Inventor, Create Value

Goals
Reality
Options
Who Will Win When
Tracking
Help

PAIDBACK - Leader, Deliver Value

Planning
Action
Interest, Ingenuity, Intention
Desire
Benefits
Advantages
Connection
Knowledge

PROTECT - Manager, Manage Value

Process
Risk, Reporting and Relations
Operations
Tactics
Employees
Capital (not just cash)
Time

The Entrepreneur Driver

CASH – Financial Capital

Capital
Assessment
Streams
Hedge

Introduction

If we want our organisations to drive forward and seek opportunity through chaos, then we must invest in developing our people to think like entrepreneurs. We need entrepreneur cultures where people think like entrepreneurs. At first this seems like an impossible task. However, I've done the work for you and made it simple, there are just 4 steps. Because there are just four secrets, we can find these in the mnemonics ORGANISE, GROWTH, PAIDBACK & PROTECT.

Entrepreneurs and Intrapreneurs

Throughout this book we will refer to both entrepreneurs and intrapreneurs. Essentially both have virtually the same reference here in that it means a system of thinking or a mindset. The main difference of course is entrepreneurs absorb the risk or the cost of an entrepreneur decision whereas intrapreneurs have a cultural fit where values are aligned with the entrepreneurs founding efforts, in short, intrapreneurs support the organisational goals and help to maintain market position while benefitting from a culture of creativity and recognition.

Why

To develop inimitable competitive advantage, we must tap into the latent entrepreneur capital in the minds of our people, we must help them to think more like entrepreneurs! Through my extensive research and by looking at entrepreneurs with a different mindset I found some amazing new ideas that help build entrepreneur skills and help people think entrepreneurially.

How

I thought the best way to enhance our thinking about entrepreneurs is to explore our knowledge of entrepreneurs, the entrepreneur environment, and entrepreneur action and consider our knowledge gaps and then model the results to raise our normal thinking to the thinking patterns of entrepreneurs.

Once we understand what entrepreneurs do and how they do it we can begin to think like an entrepreneur ourselves and develop our people to think like entrepreneurs within an organisational environment. Our people will become more entrepreneurial and our culture more intrapreneurial.

Through my scientific research published in 2011, I found high interest in entrepreneurship and high desire to be entrepreneurial amongst 450 employees. I also, found that entrepreneurs have 4 dominant roles. They spot an opportunity and identify the resources needed, they innovate and provide solutions, find a way to motivate people to achieve results and then manage the venture rewards. I found that entrepreneurs are Coordinators, Inventors, Leaders and Managers.

Entrepreneurs pursue value, they identify value, create value, deliver value and protect value in order to provide solutions or make a profit. So, to think like an entrepreneur we must think like a coordinator, inventor, leader and manager.

Entrepreneurs Roles and Value	
Coordinators	Identify Value
Inventors	Create Value
Leaders	Deliver Value
Mangers	Protect Value

Complexity

The complexity of entrepreneur thinking is apparent when we understand that each individual entrepreneur is unique, has a dominant pattern (coordinator, inventor, leader and manager) with the other roles being less dominant. This means we can be an entrepreneur leader but also have the ability of an inventor to innovate and a manager to protect and manage rewards and a coordinator to organise resources and using all these skills exploit opportunity.

For example, Albert Einstein who is widely regarded as an inventor saw himself first as an entrepreneur able to recognise constraints and spot an opportunity and inventing simply provided the vehicle for entrepreneurship. Einstein himself recognised that an entrepreneur has different roles with inventing being just one purpose. Therefore, an entrepreneur can be one person wearing many hats or an entrepreneur team but all the entrepreneur roles (coordinator, inventor, leader, manager) must be actively carried out or there won't be growth.

Entrepreneurs spot an opportunity and bring together necessary resources as a 'coordinator'. Innovation is the role of entrepreneur as an 'inventor.' Motivating people to move from a place of dissatisfaction to a more satisfying place is the role of the entrepreneur as 'leader'. The entrepreneur as manager protects all the rewards that are a consequence of the venture.

In the Negative

Without coordinators we will be disorganised, without inventors there will be no new ideas, without leaders there will be no motivation and no results, and without managers there will be no control of the venture rewards meaning the business is unlikely to survive.

Entrepreneur Teams

By conjecture, well rounded experienced entrepreneurs or entrepreneur teams are expected to have experience of identifying value through opportunity recognition, creating value through innovation, delivering value through leadership and protecting value through management of venture rewards.

KISS – Keep Intrapreneurship Simple Stupid

I have no doubt that on the surface, entrepreneurship is a sea of mystery, it's currents are extremely complex and little understood and because of this, researchers are refraining from diving in to explore its depths. However, if we are to reach out to people and encourage entrepreneurship we must understand, entrepreneur thinking and make it simple from the top all the way down to the bottom. I think I have started some ripples on the surface.

Roles Tasks & Secrets

My research into entrepreneurship has helped me to discover 4 roles, identify the 4 tasks and to find two types of motivation and entrepreneur. With this new knowledge I found 4 new tools of entrepreneurship I call the 4 secrets of entrepreneurship. Here are the roles, tasks and secrets.

Four Roles

Coordinator	Inventor	Leader	Manager

Four Tasks

Identify Value	Create Value	Deliver Value	Protect Value
Inspiration	Innovation	Motivation	Protection

Four Secrets

The 4 secrets can be found in the mnemonics ORGANISE, GROWTH, PAIDBACK, PROTECT.

ORGANISE	GROWTH	PAIDBACK	PROTECT
Opportunity	Goals	Planning	Process
Resources	Reality	Action	Risk, Reporting
Growth	Options	Interest,	and Relations
Achievement	Who Will Win	Ingenuity,	Operations
Niche or Not	When	Intention	Tactics
Improvise	Tracking	Desire	Employees
Stress-	Help	Benefits	Capital (not
tolerance		Advantages	just cash)
Exploitation		Connection	Time
		Knowledge	

The Interaction of Roles, Tasks and Secrets

Entrepreneur Roles tasks & Secrets Matrix

Entrepreneur Roles, Tasks & Secrets		
Coordinators	Identify Value	ORGANISE
Inventors	Create Value	GROWTH
Leaders	Deliver Value	PAIDBACK
Managers	Protect Value	PROTECT

With focus on the roles, tasks and tools of entrepreneurship there is a higher probability we can influence entrepreneur thinking and development of intrapreneurs within our organisations irrespective of whether we think entrepreneurs are born or made.

Capital

And not forgetting the special role of Financial Capital:

Capital	Financial Value	CASH

But also.

Entrepreneur Capital – the value of experience, knowledge, business
Intellectual Capital – the value attributed to the ability to coordinate opportunity
Human Capital – the value of the ideas, processes, opportunities in our minds
Structural Capital – the value of our systems and processes that provide scale
Network Capital – the value of relationships, reputation, credibility to perform

Analysing Entrepreneur Action

Let's start with entrepreneurs and what they do.

Entrepreneurs identify a problem, find a solution, weigh up the odds of making a profit from the product or service exploitation and then invest, manage and secure the venture rewards.

This means entrepreneurs discover ideas, find solutions, achieve results and secure gains. This is how I found the 4 secrets to entrepreneurs and developed the process to enhance entrepreneur skills within organisations using the 4 easy mnemonics:

- ORGANISE
- GROWTH
- PAIDBACK
- PROTECT

These 4 mnemonics naturally occurring help us to understand the process of entrepreneur thinking. This means we can experience the process of entrepreneur thinking and be innovative to create value, find ways to leverage resources and deliver value and secure gains to protect value. Through understanding the process of human events, we can teach the process to others and the more competent we become the greater the potential leverage.

By conjecture, the more familiar we become with entrepreneur skills, the more credible our personality, the more likely we will identify an opportunity, create intrapreneur cultures and the more probable the venture will survive, investors are more likely to lend to us and suppliers and customers are highly likely to want to do business with us. Potentially, entrepreneur thinking and intrapreneur programmes are 'a recipe for success'. There has been a growth in consultancies offering some form of 'entrepreneur thinking course' or an 'intrapreneurship event' throughout the world. Has there been economic growth as a result?

Throughout this book about 'Entrepreneur Thinking, I will provide an insight into entrepreneurs and what they do and ask the question if we know the ingredients of what makes an entrepreneur can we model their behaviour to a high enough degree that creates more entrepreneurs, more new products and more jobs.

The final pages will examine the 'born or made' scenario often associated with the subject of entrepreneurs and is only there because readers will expect some reference of this traditional argument. This research demonstrates entrepreneur skills, whether attributed to born or made, can be identified and improved upon thus, pushing the boundaries of the 'born or made' debate. However, the main point is that there are entrepreneurs, prepared to risk their time and money. In a born or made debate people are reluctant to change their point of view for fear of losing an argument!

It would be simplistic to state we can train people to be entrepreneurs, we can't, and this is because the ultimate decision involves taking a risk. However, we can train people to think like entrepreneurs and develop entrepreneur skills that can be utilised within teams inside intrapreneur cultures. This may or may not encourage the 'entrepreneur leap'.

However, we know becoming an entrepreneur is a result of many things such as an idea, resources and relations coming together at a time where the opportunity is seized and exploited. Ideally, we want to be able to spot an opportunity and take advantage of it, without too much risk and uncertainty and to survive without loss of investment. Hopefully, we can demonstrate some of the skills necessary to improve the chance of successful entrepreneur ventures and understand the steps an organisation and individuals can take to improve the economic contribution of people as entrepreneurs within organisations.

So, 'Entrepreneur Thinking aims to develop intrapreneurs and examines entrepreneurship to find the entrepreneur skills we need, to recognise an opportunity, to be innovative, to find a way to leverage an opportunity far beyond what normal people would expect and to ensure the entrepreneur and the intrapreneurs receive the rewards from the business venture. Easy!

Definition

Definition of Entrepreneur:

After finding over 250 definitions of entrepreneurship I started to look at these definitions for some sort of pattern. I quickly noticed that although there are many definitions of entrepreneurs the definitions contained many of the same words and context. For instance, some referred to the entrepreneur such as leadership or management or innovation and others to what an entrepreneur does such as achieves, motivates, coordinates, takes the profit from risk and so on. By plotting the components of the definitions, I found there were 57 words that described entrepreneurs in these definitions that were repeated.

On further scrutiny, I noticed other patterns emerging, innovation came up a lot so did leadership and manager. Many of the words also had the same or similar meaning, for example innovation and inventor, leader and achievements, manager, and coordinate. I started to group similar words together and eventually found 3 headings, inventor, leader, and manager.

I remembered watching Lord Bilimoria (Cobra Beer) talking to Peter Jones (Dragon's Den) and saying what entrepreneurs do.

Lord Bilimoria said that:

'entrepreneurs have an idea, want to take it somewhere and against all the odds making it happen!'

I came to realise that these are the roles of an entrepreneur, Inventor, Leader and Manager. Then I realised that someone must pull all of the roles together, coordinate the entrepreneur roles, so I removed coordinator, and this became the 4th entrepreneur role. We now have four entrepreneur roles:

Coordinator
Inventor
Leader
Manager

Everyone has some qualities for all of these entrepreneur roles, but one role will always be more dominant than others. The make-up of an entrepreneurial team should consist of an inventor responsible for creating value, a leader responsible for delivering value and a manager who protects value. A lone entrepreneur may perform all the roles.

My Simplest Definition of an Entrepreneur

"An entrepreneur discovers ideas, achieves results by exploiting opportunity and protects rewards".

An entrepreneur improves their value where they are able to recognise, understand and master the management of the ability to discover, achieve and protect. Improve these entrepreneur skills and increase your entrepreneur capabilities, this may lead to opportunity recognition, an entrepreneur leap and venture success with financial support based on your entrepreneur credibility.

Thus, by conjecture, 'every entrepreneur has the right to the rewards of [their] entrepreneurial creativity as a result of natural law as this create and reward cycle provides incentives and drives entrepreneur activity'. Moreover, the above principle is universal in that it can be applied to all people at all possible times in all conceivable places.'

Therefore, governments have a duty to actively support the development and growth of entrepreneur ventures in a balanced manner rather than a biased approach in favour of employment. Clearly there is an imbalance where people are driven toward employment, and this may be because we understand the job market better than entrepreneurship.

Entrepreneur Definition: Linking Roles, Value, Ingredients and Skills

So far it seems that entrepreneurs both take from society while also contributing to growth. A good friend Pascal Rodmacq tells me that there should be a word 'Donorpreneur' (the one who gives) to complement the 'entrepreneur' (the one who takes). We must, therefore, not only define the entrepreneur as a risk-taker and somebody able to take advantage of and adapt to unexpected situations, but also somebody who obtains profit by combining factors of production within the framework of a market that provides social benefits.

Purely professional activities, however profitable, are not entrepreneurial. This is why we think that a pure manager is not a real entrepreneur, but rather a professional (intrapreneur). This view of entrepreneur and entrepreneurship is not new; however, our evaluation and conclusions direct a new conceptual model of entrepreneurship by applying entrepreneurial process to entrepreneurship itself!

Understanding entrepreneurship as a process begins with a definition, developing and learning a process but ends with successful entrepreneur action.

We have found that there are 4 entrepreneur roles and as such any definition of an entrepreneur should include the roles of coordinator, inventor, leader and manager.

Definition, Entrepreneur Process and Leverage

To reach a definition we can summarise the research so far.

- A Coordinator organises entrepreneur value that is comprised of people, process networks and cash. A useful tool for Coordinators is the mnemonic ORGANISE.
- An Inventor's resource is people and their problems, issues, constraints, ideas, know-how, knowledge and experience. Inventors discover solutions and create value; we can use the GROWTH mnemonic to drive and exploit our innovation.
- A Leader manages business structure such as processes, systems, motivations and the means of achievement. Leaders achieve and get PAIDBACK.
- A Manager protects all the venture rewards that flow as a result of the business, and this includes tangible assets and intangible assets such as relationships as well as cash. Use mnemonic

PROTECT.

- Financial leverage is provided by turnover, profits, loans and investment. We use the mnemonic CASH to drive finance as a lever.

At last, I think I have a conclusive definition of an entrepreneur. Based on all the academic and practical information I have gathered; on analysis this is my definition of an entrepreneur:

> *'An entrepreneur is someone who recognises, understands and masters the management of resources (coordinator). Resources include people (inventor), process (leader) networks (manager) and cash' to provide a benefit to mankind that can be exploited.*

Having identified the entrepreneur roles, I still needed to find the tasks entrepreneurs actually do but reaching the definition of an entrepreneur thanks to the wisdom of Lord Bilimoria is a great start. I needed to make further discoveries and moved to look at the types of entrepreneurs and their environments.

Entrepreneur Environment Matrix

	Entrepreneur		
Solus	**Driven by Personal Physiological wants and needs**	**Driven by Solutions that Benefit Mankind**	**Social**
	Job that pays a wage	**Makes decisions in someone else's business**	
	Intrapreneur		

Driven by money or driven by solutions?

Entrepreneur Types

I needed a strategy to determine the types of entrepreneurs, so I looked at entrepreneurs and their possible motivations and found two money or solutions.

Solus

What motivates an entrepreneur to start a venture and take an investment risk? There are only two reasons why anyone would risk time and money. The first is simple, to make more money and some entrepreneurs are motivated to just make money. I call this entrepreneur the 'Solus' entrepreneur. This is because the decisions a Solus entrepreneur makes are to make money for personal reasons and there is little if any social benefit to the wider community. The extreme Solus may be criminal or murderer acting only for internally driven selfish or even psychotic reasons. However, we are concerned here with entrepreneurs who might be sole operators providing for family wants and needs or driven organisation's for example the pile it high sell it cheap wheeler dealer type who spots an opportunity to buy cheap, sell fast and make a quick profit.

Social

On the other hand, we have the entrepreneur who first sees a problem to solve for the benefit of mankind and by providing the solution this entrepreneur will make money but it's not the driver, solutions are. I call this entrepreneur the 'Social' entrepreneur because the aim of a social entrepreneur is to benefit mankind. The extreme Social entrepreneur is the philanthropist who gives time and money to help mankind for example to rid the world of disease or some other social ill. However, we are interested in the Social entrepreneur who sees an opportunity to provide a solution and making money is not the primary driver although it is an important one. Solution driven entrepreneurs may include examples such as Google, Dyson, Apple, Cats Eyes, Ring Pull, and the light bulb.

Solus Entrepreneur	Social Entrepreneur
Driven by Personal Physiological Wants and Needs	Driven by Solutions that Benefit Mankind
Solus Intrapreneur	**Social Intrapreneur**
Makes an investment in someone else's idea or process	Makes decisions in someone else's business but does not invest their own money

Intrapreneur

There are two types of intrapreneur, Solus and Social again. A Social intrapreneur makes decisions in someone else's business but does not invest their own money. A Solus intrapreneur makes an investment in someone else's idea or process.

The Ingredients of the Entrepreneur as Coordinator

Entrepreneur as Coordinator

The person who brings it all together and identifies value

Coordinator Role & Tasks

Let's look at entrepreneurs in the context of the statement from Lord Bilimoria. It's mandatory to expect someone to pull everything together so the entrepreneur as a coordinator that organises resources is easily justifiable. Resources include everything required to make the venture viable and will include the means of production, people, money and machinery and tools etc. Building a positive work culture where people want to stay and contribute is not an easy task. People need to be appreciated and too much focus on business objectives can leave the people who deliver the value the business craves may not want to hang around if their needs are ignored. However, the coordinator must be aware of why businesses fail for example 47% of businesses fail because there is no identified market need for the product or service, therefore prudent coordinator may have as a top priority to conduct a market gap analysis.

Definition: Entrepreneur Coordinator

The entrepreneur coordinator is someone who, spots an opportunity, sees the big picture and recognises the tangible and intangible resources required to solve the problem, overcome barriers and produce a solution that can be leveraged and scaled to return a profit and economic growth in an organised way.

A Coordinator

Develops
Advises
Supervises
Organises

Entrepreneur as Coordinator	
ORGANISE	
Opportunity	Recognition from a Big Picture perspective
Resource	Identify tangible/intangible assets to achieve aims
Growth	Scale production by creating new systems and procedures
Achievement	Collaborate resources and teams to pull together the vision
Niche or not	Where to start. Niche or adapt, copy, imitate
Improvise	Innovate and bricolage (using whatever is at hand)
Stress-tolerant	To reach Harmonious Finality in difficult environments
Exploitation	Drive marketing strategies to return a profit margin

ORGANISE

- Opportunity
- Resource
- Growth
- Achievement
- Niche or Not
- Improvise
- Stress-tolerant
- Exploitation

Opportunity Recognition from a Big Picture perspective
Resource identification, tangible and intangible assets that will achieve the aims
Growth and scale production by creating new systems, policies and procedures
Achievement Collaborate resources and teams to pull together the vision
Niche or Not, deciding on the type of market for the product
Improvise, innovate and bricolage (using whatever is at hand)
Stress tolerant to reach 'Harmonious Finality' in difficult environments
Exploit Opportunity for Profit

Opportunity Recognition

Entrepreneurs have the ability of recognition of business ideas and opportunities from a 'Big Picture' perspective and to spot an opportunity in an instant, often referred to as 'Entrepreneur flash'. So, what happens here? Ideas and opportunities invariably originate from people's problems. People need to do something or want a solution to a problem they face, it could be too hot, too cold, too slow, too fast or whatever it is they want or need they are prepared to pay for so that they can move from a place of dissatisfaction to a more pleasant place. In effect entrepreneurs take away the pain of the problem and move customers to a more pleasurable place, it's the old hedonistic pain and pleasure scenario. We don't like pain and we are prepared to pay for solutions that remove the pain. So, entrepreneurs see the issue, problem or constraint (Reality), they recognise the standard that will satisfy the customer (Goals), they consider possible means of resolving the problem and achieving the standard (Options), They put in place a winning team that will deliver the product or services and relieve the pain that the customer will pay for (Who Will Win When). This is an innovation process and understanding how innovation works means a steady flow of entrepreneur ideas.

Resources

Identify tangible/intangible assets to achieve aims.

Help, advice, support
Mentors, industry experts
Knowledge, education
Employees
Money, Investment

Nurturing & Mentors

Arguably, spending quality resources in nurturing programmes will create a more confident and knowledgeable base of entrepreneurs. The government already has mentoring systems, but these are in need of improvement to raise the chances of venture success in the first year where statistics show around 50% of businesses regularly fail and 95% fail by year 5. These figures are unacceptably high and much more support is necessary but it's crystal clear that a radical change is necessary, as the old way simply does not provide anywhere near acceptable results. Mentors: how successful are they, what structure do they follow and how useful is the statistical data.

Funding

Identify income streams early
Choice - student loan or start up loan.
Family loans
Credit cards or unsecured loans
Start-up loans, Bank loans or (Government loans e.g., NEA)
Supplier credit terms
Remove red tape to encourage innovation
Tax breaks
VAT concessions
Financial help for new employees

Networks

Identifying relationships to leverage opportunity of early returns.
Relationships build goodwill so focus should be on increasing reputation and credibility.
Leverage the mentor's knowledge to determine best suppliers, cost price and selling price, retail outlets, sales systems,

Entrepreneur Referents
Where there is the right entrepreneur environment there will be no barriers only drivers.
Great idea
Solution to Benefit mankind
Know-how
Business relationships
Family support
Family to support
Lost job
Redundancy pay
Lottery winnings
Cash windfall
Inheritance

Growth

Entrepreneur ventures are different to self-employment because they think big and as such aim for exponential growth.

Leverage

Leverage resources by adding processes and replicate success.

Scale

We need to be able to scale the business or it won't grow. Scale production by creating new systems and procedures

Achievement (Vision)

Creating a vision. Collaborate resources and teams to pull together the vision.

Drivers

- Great idea.
- A winning attitude.
- Money.
- Motivation.

Barriers

There are 4 primary barriers, business knowledge, business regulations, finance, and personal circumstances. Entrepreneurs must think of ways that these barriers can be overcome. The barriers are different for each entrepreneur, some will have the money to start, and others will need loans or investors, others will be more familiar with business efficacies and regulations than new entrepreneurs and personal circumstances

Niche or Not

Where to start? Innovate, adapt or improvise.

But I Don't Have an Idea for a Business

94% of businesses are nothing new they take an ordinary idea and innovate, adapt or improvise the products or services to make something exceptional. A great example is the Dyson approach to the vacuum cleaner, a new design to an age-old cleaning problem. Now, what are the problems with the Dyson Cleaner and how can we make it better?

Where to Start-up – Niche?

What is a niche market and how do I find one?

A niche market is a market where a portion of the market is targeted or focused on.

The motor industry provides some good examples, instead of providing garage services a niche market may be:

Electrical fault diagnosis and repairs
Tyres
Alloy wheel refurbishment
Car wash
Executive Valet
Car breakers

Etc.

A niche market may be best described as a specialised service or product for a narrowly defined group of customers.

How do we find a niche market?

Discovering niche markets requires hard work, an eye for opportunity and the ability to provide solutions.

The best place to start is to consider the industry that we are familiar with and perform a comprehensive market analysis and then focus on gap analysis models.

A market analysis will identify market uncertainties. Uncertainty means there are risks and this means opportunity. Where there is a known risk, this can be offset, and the opportunity exploited. This opportunity is a niche market.

For example: in the motor industry the trend for gas guzzling off-road vehicles may be interrupted where political unrest or an economic downturn forces up the price of fuel. Budgets may be squeezed and as a result consumers demand more fuel-efficient cars. This is a niche market, manufacturers who are fast to respond to market demands can take advantage and exploit the niche.

Other examples of niche market may include cleaning services that specialise in hotel linen, wedding dresses, domestic carpets etc.

Tech companies and bio companies demonstrate how knowledge from one industry can be used to provide incredibly smart solutions. This can mean applying Nano technology or anaerobic solutions or a transfer of materials such as making clothes from recycled materials.

Finding the niche is the first step, the next step is asking customers what they want and need from the product and then applying knowledge to develop the right product and service.

Niche markets can be extremely profitable but speed to market is key to success as very quickly there will be competitors.

Niche markets are waiting to be found and having a process of niche market discovery will help provide competitive advantage for keen, hungry business entrepreneurs.

Improvise

Innovate and bricolage (using whatever is at hand)

Applications of techniques to discover solutions include:

Engineering
Re-engineering
Reverse-engineering

This means:

Innovating – Coming up with something entirely new!
Adapting – Making an existing solution better, faster, cheaper, stronger etc
Improvising – Using a solution in a way it was never intended to be used

Entrepreneur Toolkit

ORGANISE, GROWTH, PAIDBACK, PROTECT, CASH

Entrepreneur skills in Practice

The ability to discover, achieve and protect. Simply put entrepreneur definitions focus on inventing, leading and managing. Therefore, key skills should focus on the discovery of ideas, achieving results and managing the venture value.

These key skills should be wrapped around our normal education systems. This will provide a habitual grounding in practical entrepreneur skills unleashing an ambition of potential entrepreneurs.

It is with interest that we have observed entrepreneurs give up a business to go to college, other entrepreneurs who want to work in a business and the many employees who want to be entrepreneurs! Is it a case of the grass is greener?

Having the skills is a wonderful start and leaping into entrepreneur action, well that's a personal decision! And, money, value, experience and know-how, well, entrepreneurs are either born with this type of capital or they make their own.

Stress-Tolerant

To reach 'Harmonious Finality' in very difficult environments we must set goals and find a means to achieve them.

Entrepreneur Mindset - Seek out constraints.
Entrepreneur Spirit – A can do attitude

Exploitation

Drive marketing strategies to return a profit margin. Success does not depend upon having the best idea or the most money. Success often results from the way in which the idea is brought to market. The extraordinary means of executing an ordinary idea that meets the consumer's needs such as fashion, versatility, cheaper, faster or more durable.

Business Case

We should conduct a gap analysis that demonstrates the business fills a market need.

The business case is the reason we are in business and is normally a formal document with an intention to gain investment support, acquire business resources or prove credibility.

The business case should simply present the facts, the opportunity, the probability of success, the necessary investment and the expected returns and the business benefits and risks.

For example, a high street furniture store doesn't make enough money on a Friday evening to cover operational costs, however, a marketing strategy will increase operational costs but also sales and presenting this fact to the storeowner may be a great reason to increase marketing budgets.

The business case should demonstrate the difference between deciding against the action or taking the action and the conclusion must be a compelling argument to implement the recommendations.

Business Recipe

Why we are in business: Viability, Demand, and Strategy.

Our business recipe identifies the strengths and purpose of the company in terms of knowledge, experience and vision. The vision must align everyone in the company and each person must understand how he or she fit in.

Having identified exploitable constraints and developed a market opportunity the business recipe identifies the strategy and tactics that will exploit the opportunity for profit.

Market viability:

Is there a market and need for the product or service? We should conduct an external analysis of market size, our target customer, the market segment and potential barriers to entry and survival.

Customer Demand:

Most businesses fail because there is no identified market for the product. The first steps are to ensure the product really does solve a problem. This means identifying the customer's 'needs' or creating customer 'wants'. Then is the product a suitable solution to the customer's wants or needs. Consider the amount of customers who need to purchase the product to make the business viable and at what price must the product be sold at to cover the costs and make a profit. Are there other similar products that solve the customer's problem and meet their wants and needs and why would customers switch to your product, for example, is it cheaper, faster or more reliable.

Strategy:

Strategic objectives, what we need to achieve.
Tactical objectives, the tactics we will employ to achieve strategic objectives.

We need to know how everything fits together, how it is supposed to work and the returns we expect to achieve. We can build a simple model to provide a snapshot of our people, process and networks to determine how we make money and discover if this is efficient. Thereafter we can explore other new ways to find exponential growth.

Using our GROWTH model (explained later) we can ask open questions that help determine where we are in the context of the business recipe. Where we want to be in future. What actions we need to take to ensure we meet our objectives and what are the potential risks and contingencies we need to plan that may prevent the delivery of the business recipe.

Focus on Entrepreneur Needs

- Coordinating resources using the ORGANISE Model
- Discover solutions using the GROWTH Model
- Achieving objectives using the PAIDBACK Model
- Protecting rewards using the PROTECT Model
- Managing financial capital using the CASH Model

Some Questions:

Who are the key employees to delivering our business recipe?
What actions are we taking to ensure key employee retention?
What are the key competencies required to deliver on the business recipe.
How do we rate the ability of each person to deliver on the business recipe?
How do we rate the processes in delivering on the business recipe?

What margins are we expecting to make?
How will people and processes be appraised in achieving set margins?
How will the appraisal system be measured in improving margins?

What are the effects of key relationships on business performance?

Do our people have the required competencies to be able to compete?
What is our ability to compete in the future?

How often will processes be reviewed to avoid adverse trends?
Can we improve on review and monitoring of performance?

How will business relationships be formed and maintained?
Can we do more to build relationships?

What training and development strategies are in place?
Can we meet the demands of inevitable change in future business landscapes?

What are the risks to employees, processes and relationships?
What is the result of losing customers?
What actions can we take to ensure we retain our customers?

Then "Benchmark' the business against industry and non-industry competitors to establish disposable income available for your products or services.

It is very important that positive action is a result and directly attributable to the internal analysis. Our analysis focuses on opportunity recognition, discovering solutions, achieving objectives and protecting rewards within budgetary constraints.

Strategic Plans

Ideally, we should plan everything and measure everything using a mix of strategic and tactical objectives. Strategic what we are planning to achieve and tactical how we will achieve the strategy. There must be a means to measure progress and ensure we stay on track to achieve what we set out to achieve within budget and deadlines.

Quantifiable Objectives

Measuring tangibles is much easier we just count them.
Aim to increase sales conversions from 5% to 10% by the end of quarter 4.

Qualitative Objectives

Measuring intangibles, non-financial measures or personality measures is much more difficult. There are no accurate ways to measure qualitative objectives. However, we can measure intangibles or goodwill and be consistent by using the "Paul Clargo Goodwill Scale" which is a combination of $Y = Fx2$ and the training matrix expressed as a percentage of 100. This will provide a measurement based on ingredients and a logical measure.

Aim to develop the performance of salesperson 'x' to be able to achieve the company standards of performance by end of quarter 4.

Example:

Ingredients	*	*	*	*
Product Knowledge				X
Presentation skills		X		
Total as a %				**75%**

Using the same system of analysis will mean consistency of results and a greater understanding of the company and the person or non-financial measure that is being assessed. Simple.

Tactical Objectives

The things we will do to achieve the strategic objectives.

Entrepreneur as Coordinator (Summary)

Entrepreneur as Coordinator		
ORGANISE	Entrepreneur Thinking	Entrepreneur Action
Opportunity	Recognition from a Big Picture perspective	Opportunity Recognition Entrepreneur Flash Business Ideas
Resource	Identify tangible/intangible assets to achieve aims	Help, advice, support Mentors, industry experts Knowledge, education Employees, Networks Money, Investment
Growth	Scale production by creating new systems and procedures	Leverage & Scale
Achievement	Collaborate resources and teams to pull together the vision	Drivers & Barriers Creating a vision Overcoming barriers
Niche or not	Where to start - Niche	Niche, adapt, copy, imitate
Improvise	Innovate and bricolage (using whatever is at hand)	Entrepreneur Toolkit Key Skills
Stress-tolerant	To reach Harmonious Finality in difficult environments	Entrepreneur Mindset Can do attitude
Exploitation	Drive marketing strategies to return a profit margin	Business Case Business Recipe Strategic Plans

The Ingredients of Entrepreneur as Inventor

Entrepreneur as Inventor

The Ideas person

Creates Value

Inventor Roles

Dominant Role as Entrepreneur Inventor is to Discover opportunity
Secondary Roles as Entrepreneur Inventor/Leader is to move projects forward
Secondary Roles as Entrepreneur Inventor/Manager is to control resources

Inventor Role & Tasks

In order to understand the inventor role, I looked at what happens in entrepreneurship and having regard to what Lord Bilimoria said I thought about an inventor having an idea and how an idea comes about. I found ideas start from some kind of an issue, constraint or problems that prevent people from doing something. This could be anything from travelling, eating, keeping warm or cold, running, walking, entering into a legal contract and a million other things. When people need to do something and can't, there is an opportunity to solve the problem and possibly sell the solution. If we can sell the solution, there is an opportunity for growth. (We will see more of GROWTH later). Entrepreneurs as inventors are always thinking of issues, problems and constraints for which they can generate a solution that people will buy and create value.

Entrepreneur Inventors Discover

What an entrepreneur inventor does

Entrepreneurs as Inventors discover, they find problems, issues and constraints that cause us pain and look for the solutions that provide pleasure and an opportunity to exploit the solution or service for gain. By doing this, entrepreneurs as inventors, create value. Entrepreneurs say they do this mental analysis in an instant and I call it the entrepreneur spark that ignites the idea and creativity that results from the initial idea. One of the most famous inventors was Albert Einstein. However, while people see Einstein as an inventor, Einstein saw himself as an entrepreneur first, he said the inventions just gave him the opportunity to be entrepreneurial. Ideas provide growth and we can use the GROWTH model to drive innovation and develop ideas and solutions in a structured way.

GROWTH is Goals, Reality, Who Will Win When, Tracking & Help.

GROWTH

Start with our reality, e.g., what is really going on in our business? What are the issues we face? Who is having problems, is it customers, suppliers or employees? Write down everything. At this first stage don't try to solve anything, focus only on the reality of the current circumstances. Once we know where we are we can identify the standards we would expect to achieve, these become our realistic goals. Having realistic goals allows us to find the means to achieve these goals.

Entrepreneur GROWTH		
Inventor Role	**Resources**	**Strategy**
Discover	Human Capital	GROWTH
Create	Constraints	Goals
Innovate	Problems	Reality
Adapt	Ideas	Options
Improvise	Solutions	Who Will Win When
Engineer	Money	Tracking
Re-engineer	Tools	Help
Reverse-Engineer	Plat & Machinery	

Goals

GROWTH is a system for delivering value through innovation. This is how we leverage human capital, the ideas in our heads.

The first part of GROWTH is Goals
Goals identify the standards we set for our company, our products and our people.

Vision
Mission
Purpose
Primary aims
Primary goals
Strategic objectives
Tactical objectives

Vision

A vision statement helps focus on how the organisation aims to look and be like in the near and distant future and is usually written by the senior managers. The aim is to focus group thinking beyond the daily activities toward distant objectives.

Mission

The mission describes what business the organisation is in (and what it isn't) both now and projecting into the future. Its aim is to provide focus for management and staff.

Values & Principles

Values describe the desired culture and help shape organisational culture.

Principles focus on providing employees with directions or core values.

Purpose

The purpose of the business is what we actually do that benefits customers. I prefer a 'Mantra" . For example, find 3 words that describe what your company does that will instantly resonate with your customer, a burger company may say ' we sell burgers', that's it. It's motivational, easy to remember and tells customers exactly what they get from your company.

Primary aims

The high level strategy we will implement to achieve the vision e.g., for a retailer this may mean establishing channels of distribution on key retail sites.

Primary goals

How we will achieve the primary aims, e.g., for a retailer this will mean specific retail parks, target landlords, securing tenure at best prices etc Strategic objectives

What we will do to achieve the business goals, for the retailer this may involve specific products tailored for the target market segment

Tactical objectives

The tactics we will employ to drive business success, here the retailer will focus on hyper-competition, promotional offers, staff training, partners etc

Reality

The advantage of GROWTH is it helps find solutions to problems we may not even be aware of. Therefore, to determine our reality we must identify constraints.

Constraints prevent us achieving the standards we set for our company, our products and our people. To identify constraints, we analyse what's happening inside and outside the business. Focus only on what's wrong, don't try and solve anything at this stage. Complete a thorough business analysis.

Think of constraints as a network opportunity.

- Analyse the current position, aim for complete transparency
- List Points for discussion
- Gather comprehensive details of constraints, problems, issues affecting the business
- Be mindful not to search for solutions at this stage, but do make notes for later stages
- Ask open Questions (who, what, where, why, when & how) eg:
- What is happening in the organisation at present?
- What's wrong with it?
- How can we do it better?
- What does the customer want?
- What does the customer need?

Internal

Business idea & drivers of change:

Political -
Economical
Social
Technological
Legal
Environmental

Benchmarking: Compare our-selves against the industry and other competition.

Balance Audit:

Ability to compete – Do we have the competencies necessary to compete or can we get them?
Value for money – Can we produce the product or service at a competitive price
Resources – Do we have the resources to deliver the product or service cost-effectively?

HIPER – Drivers

Hackers – Businesses trying to steal your secrets and your market share
Imitations – Cheaper products that copy or adapt or fake your idea
Power of Networks – Full transparency of relations, buyers, suppliers, customers
Exit – Always Be in Control, have a contingency to grow or exit on your terms
Rivalry – Can be internal as well as external

HIPER Drivers

HIPER – Drivers

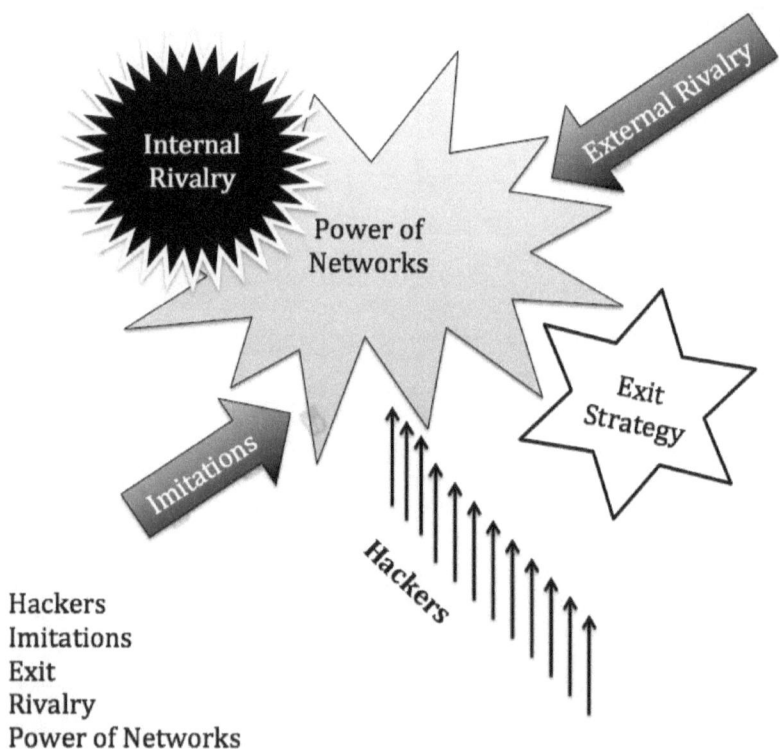

Hackers
Imitations
Exit
Rivalry
Power of Networks

Income Streams

Gold mines – Steady supply and reliable.
Diamond mines – Hard to find but valuable.
Pearl Farms – Can be worthless, valuable, and priceless.
Coal mines – Need to be there, turn over cash but low profit.

Income Streams

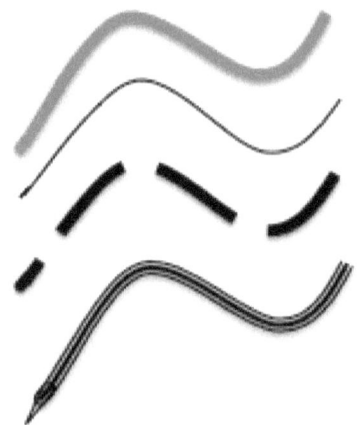

Gold

Diamonds

Pearls

Coal Mines

Identify income streams early. Generating income streams means a steady cash flow and less reliance on banks and investors and more control on the finances of the business venture.

External

BIPS & SADDS – Power of Value Networks

Everything a business does is so intertwined that it's difficult to separate the component parts as one activity always affects another. Therefore, view the business as a whole, as a network. Networks deliver value and measurable results or rewards with every activity undertaken.

BIPS

Buying
IT
People
Systems

SADDS

Sales & Operations
Advertising
Deliveries
Dispatch
Service

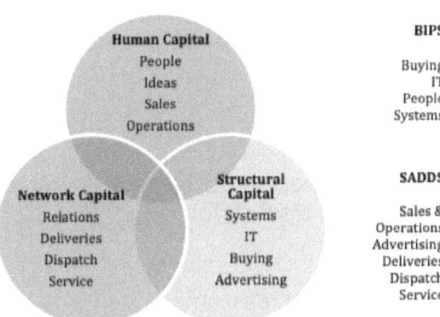

BIPS & SADDS - Power of Value Networks

Culture & Stakeholders:

Values – Consider the business values
Beliefs – What are our beliefs
Paradigm – Where are we now
Relationships - Consider our networks and relations

Visible competencies – How skilled are we as a business
Management method – What type of management strategy
Power of IT – Can we use IT to leverage resources?
Knowledge creation – Identify knowledge gaps

Strategic leadership - vital for strategy development

Power interest – Who holds the power and what level of interest do they have?
Player – Who are the players?
Control – Who has control?

SWOT – Summarise our strengths, weaknesses, opportunities and threats.

Options

GROWTH directs positive thinking toward possible options to solve problems, exploit opportunity and deliver the standards we set for our company, our products and our people.

Consider the make-up of problem solving team.
Generate possible solutions
Brainstorm & Samised
Think of strategic fit:

There are only 4 Options: Product development, Market development Consolidation/ market penetration, Diversification

Feasible – Is it feasibly achievable?
Suitable – Is it suitable within our mission statement?
Acceptable – Is it acceptable to our stakeholders?

Mission fit – does the strategy fit our mission? If not change the strategy/mission
Primary objectives fit
Strategic objectives fit
Tactical objectives fit

Summary
Considered constraints
Provided options
Ensure options meet set standards
Solutions compared against what the company is trying to achieve

Who Will Win When

GROWTH provides a structured framework that encourages teamwork and consolidated team action. Through team analysis of constraints GROWTH directs positive thinking toward the most competent person to lead the project and project team, to solve problems, exploit opportunity and deliver the standards we set for our company, our products and our people within set deadlines

- Values Alignment, commit to specific action, Confirm the Will
- Assign Tasks, Names, Roles, Responsibilities, Deadlines
- Everyone should know what needs to be done to solve the problem and achieve goals
- 'Walk the Talk', well-planned, understood, clear goals established and most of all the team must be 'willing to get things done'!
- Positive mental attitude, ability, skills, competence, confidence, trust and support, enthusiasm etc. should all be considered to ensure a high degree of team motivation.

Who Will Win When

Who – Identify Results driven leader

- **Values alignment**
- **Beliefs**
- **Principles**
- **'Must do" attitude**
- **Reliable**
- **Cost focused**
- **Gets behind the plan**
- **Team leader**

Win – Must have winning ways

- Track record of success
- Achiever type personality
- Leadership attributes
- Team motivated
- Task orientated

Will – Assess Person against the task

- **Positive Mental Attitude**
- **Enthusiasm**
- **Can do attitude**
- **Gets behind the plan**
- **Raises above setbacks to find solutions**
- **Believes in the vision**

When – A Time bound project

- Deadlines
- Targets
- Goals
- Aims
- Objectives
- Planning
- Controls
- Accountability

- Identify players - Get the best person for the job
- Align values - Stakeholders have peace of mind
- Identify objectives - Increase the probability of success
- Set deadlines - Come in on time and within budget

Tracking

GROWTH ensures tracking of project deliverables to ensure the project outcomes are achieved on time and allows correction and improvement where unfavourable variables are observed. This means there is an increased probability of project success, raising the possibility of opportunity exploitation that meets the standards we set for our company, our products and our people.

Measure - $Y = f x^2$ (identify the ingredients)
Monitor
Review
Support / correct

The 'Goodwill Measure'

Help

GROWTH ensures we consider our ability to meet project demands through assessing our core competencies against the project deliverables. Where knowledge gaps are exposed that may affect the success of a project action must be considered to rectify this or the project is destined to fail or return reduced profits for resources invested.

Summary:

- Help is a key ingredient of entrepreneurship / Ask for it
- It's important to be able to assess core competencies
- By identifying knowledge gaps, we can target the help necessary to compete
- Knowledge gaps help us develop training from internal or external sources
- Transparency of activities determines project success or failure
- Success or failure depends on quality and quantity of relevant knowledge
- Relevant knowledge means we can take corrective action early

The Entrepreneur & help

Help Me:

- Entrepreneurs make the rules, asking for help is part of the learning curve
- You want to grow fast and large, we need others to help to do this
- Scale and leverage comes from help
- Human Capital contribute ideas
- More ideas early on
- Later stages improving on old ideas
- Less new ideas as the business matures
- Help to recognise new business landscapes

HELP	
Recognition, Analysis & Action **What help do we need?** - **Can we identify our weaknesses or knowledge gaps?** - **What are the real issues?** - **Can we help ourselves?** - **Do we need external help?** - **Do we have a strategy to monitor, review and adjust?** - **What are our knowledge gaps?** - **Do we have the competencies to compete?** - **Do we need external expertise?** - **What support is required in marketing, sales, operations and finance?** - **When must we be ready, make a plan of action**	**Identify Core competencies?** - Identify the goals - Consider our attitude, knowledge, skills in relation to the task - Identify the products our customers buy - Identify the work required to achieve the goals - What are the core competencies required - What processes and relationships are needed, do we have them, can we meet the set standard etc? - How may we help ourselves achieve the goals? - Consider the help and assistance required to achieve the goals.
Internal & External Help **Internal** - **Training, Coaching, Mentoring** - **Buddy systems** - **Research and development** **External** - **Industry experts** - **Consultants** - **Training partners, Universities, Colleges** - **Tools** - **Machinery**	**Create, Deliver & Manage value.** - Focus on productivity - Focus on eradicating weaknesses - Focus on developing strengths - Prepare for uncertainty - Recognise that we may not be competent at certain activities - Identify our weaknesses and take action to improve - Prevent 'head in the sand' syndrome - Builds more talented individuals - Builds team philosophy - Increases probability of success

Example of a Help Matrix:

GROWTH and Change Management

To determine the company's position and future opportunities there are a few different options.

Employ large firm business consultants that can be expensive.
Appoint internal assessors to confirm the business viability but in all probability, this is likely to return results with some bias as the assessor may think they know the answer to a question and fail to complete a full analysis.

The Growth Model

The Growth Model	
Goals	Identify the goals. Vision, Mission, Aims, Objectives
Reality	Where are we now? What is the reality of the current situation?
Options	What options are available to us to achieve the identified goals?
Who Will Win When	Who will lead, are values aligned, Do they have the Will and values aligned, is there a Winning record, When will this happen?
Tracking	How can we measure, monitor and review progress?
Help	What specialist help do we need, now or tomorrow?

Involve the whole business in the analysis through using a purpose built and focused strategy. We will be able to tap into the deep knowledge and experiences of sharp end users. Having a process of analysis that the business can use regularly will mean everyone becomes familiar with the way things are done around here and this can become part of the culture.

The Ingredients of Entrepreneur as Leader

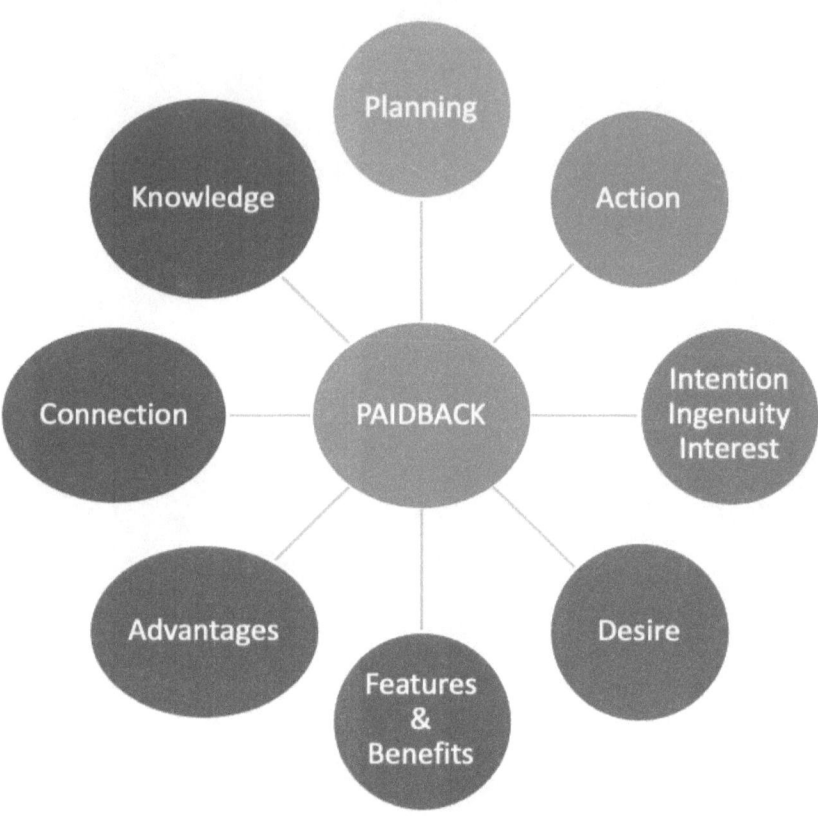

Entrepreneur as Leader

- The entrepreneur as leader motivates people to achieve results.
- Dominant role as Entrepreneur Leader is to deliver value
- Secondary Roles as Entrepreneur Leader/Inventor is to identify opportunities
- Secondary Roles as Entrepreneur Leader/Manager is to protect resources

Leader Role & Tasks

The mistake I made here was trying to differentiate the role of leader and manager. There are as many definitions about leaders and managers as there are entrepreneurs. However, when I went back to the definitions and the patterns that emerged, I was straight back on track, the entrepreneur as leader achieves results. This means that the entrepreneur leader has a vision of a better position, one that is more satisfying. However, to move from a place of dissatisfaction to a more satisfying place people must realise they are dissatisfied where they are at the moment. After which, people need to be motivated, resources found and allocated, and a plan of action agreed to achieve results.

Entrepreneurs will put their house on the line and take risks with their own money when they believe they can achieve the results they have set themselves. This acceptance of risk is how they get paid back for their initial investment after all liabilities are met. Therefore, it is of the utmost importance that the entrepreneur actions are based on sound judgment and that there is a high probability that the set goals are attainable and that the strategic and tactical objectives will achieve the plan. Entrepreneurs as leaders move dissatisfied people to a more desirable position, they deliver value and are therefore set apart from managers who have a different function, as we shall see below.

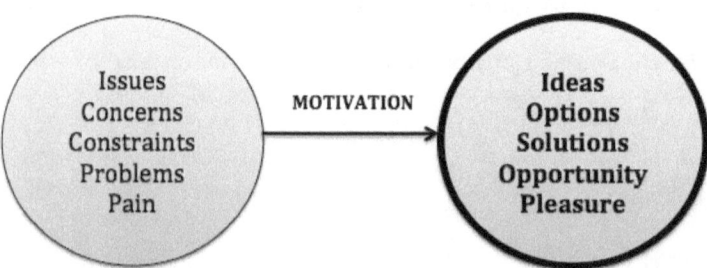

Entrepreneur Leader Motivates Action

Issues
Concerns
Constraints
Problems
Pain

MOTIVATION

Ideas
Options
Solutions
Opportunity
Pleasure

Entrepreneur Leaders Achieve

An Entrepreneur Leader acknowledges the past and recognises the dissatisfaction with the present state then creates the means to motivate people to move from the place of dissatisfaction to a more desirable position.

In hedonistic terms the Entrepreneur Leader motivates people to move from pain to pleasure. The current state is painful because we have problems however, when we move as a team toward the new goals and achieve the results there will be pleasure.

When leaders achieve, they invest both time and resources to motivate people, improve products and services, improve work practices or procedures, develop people through training and increase profit margins and return on investment. In short, entrepreneur leaders get paid back for time and investment. PAIDBACK!

The PAIDBACK Model

The PAIDBACK Model	
Planning	Plan strategic and tactical goals
Action	The planned actions and activities we will take to achieve aims
Intention **Ingenuity** **Interest**	Why we are in business (Business Case) The business unique selling proposition (USP) Why you should buy from us (Benefit Statement)
Desire	Identify 'Wants and Needs"
Benefits	Product features and benefits that fulfill 'wants and needs'
Advantages	Why customers buy The advantages to customers of buying this solution
Connection **Cheque** **Check** **Close**	Connect and build reciprocal relationships Ask for the cheque or we won't get paid Check that what you agreed is what the customer really wants Trust Credibility and Service
Knowledge	Knowledge Management What have we learned today, how can we use this tomorrow?

PAIDBACK

Entrepreneurial leaders get things done and achieve the results they have focused on. They have this in common and the great leaders of tomorrow will also get things done. They have 'Entrepreneurial Value'.

We don't remember leaders, managers, coaches or mentors that fail. It's not about personality, behavioural characteristics or anything else that psychologists or other professionals will try to tell us. The truth is that people are very complex, will react unpredictably in situations where we try to predict behaviour and psychologists are not fortunetellers. Leaders come from everywhere, but great leaders have one thing in common, they get things done. They achieve results.

Discovery	Achievement	Protecting Value
The centre-piece Economically dynamic Independent Internal locus of control Functional Decisive	Leadership Need for Achievement Driven to Succeed Process Improver Believes in Vision Motivation Exploits Opportunity Combines Manufacturing Unites production	Management attitudes Management skills Coordinates production Coordinates distribution

Leadership success means

Having a purpose.
Creating a shared vision
Developing a mission
Setting goals, aims, objectives
Deciding strategic objectives and tactics.
Ensuring the purpose of our existence is aligned with our daily actions.

To do this we need policy, procedures, systems, and process in order to succeed at a high level.

PAIDBACK is Planning, Action, Intention Interest & Ingenuity, Desire, Benefits (Features), Advantages, Connection Cheque Check, Knowledge.

PAIDBACK - Leadership & Leverage

- Planning — Start with the end in mind, the Vision
- Action — Where are we now, where do we want to be
- Ingenuity — (Interest & Intentions) – How are we going to get there
- Desire — Ask questions and make decisions
- Benefits — The reasons why we need to change
- Advantages — How change improve our position
- Connection — The motivation for acting
- Knowledge — Understanding our actions and assessing performance

PAIDBACK a Framework for success

- Planning — Focuses the mind on what must be achieved
- Action — Places leader at the centre of activity, goals & achievement
- Interest(Intention & Ingenuity) – Strategy to exploit opportunity
- Desire — Ability to ask structured questions and make decisions
- Benefits — This is how and why it works
- Advantages — This is how we will improve our position
- Connection — The 'what's in it for me' part of leadership
- Knowledge — Ensures economic, efficient & effective management

PAIDBACK & Entrepreneur Action

- Planning: Develop strategy and identify strategic steps
- Action: Identify the actions required to achieve the plan
- Intention: Tell our people what needs to be done and how to do it
- Desire: Encourage questions and meet wants and needs
- Benefits: There must be value in what we are doing to achieve results
- Advantages: Understand how change means a more pleasurable state
- Connection: Importance of people & networks to drive value delivery
- Knowledge: Must be an ever-searching quest for more

Planning

Plan elements – The steps we will take to achieve our vision
Identify our Customer – Who is our customer?
Strategy – State existing goals or establish new goals
Objectives – list all the activities we need to plan to achieve the desired results
Project management – Begin with the end in mind
Industry standards – the minimum standards we must achieve
Identified resources – the resources we have available or must acquire
Budgetary constraints / risk – the obstacles we have identified
Financial plan – The controls we will establish to ensure success

Planning for success

Without a plan we will end up somewhere we don't want to be!

Aims & Objectives

Aim:
- To recognise that we can improve our business profits without any more customers
- To understand that increasing our service increases our profits

Outcomes:

- We choose the standard & quality of service we provide
- We control our ability to improve or change our standard of service

The paidback Structured Sales Model

Paidback: Planning measures

Planning for Sales Success

- What is a plan?
- What can a plan do for you?
- The benefits of planning.
- Keeping a time log.
- Make a financial plan, cash flow forecast, spending plan
- SMART objectives.
- Measure your success against your plan.

Planning - What is a plan?

- A plan clearly identifies where you are, where you want to be and how you will get there.
- A plan helps you make decisions about situations before they occur.

What a plan can do for us

- We all plan - holidays, shopping trips, weddings and babies are good examples.
- Important to have a plan at work and to include meal breaks, holidays etc.
- Set aside time for personal development.
- Set challenging goals.
- Goals are easier achieved if you break down the tasks. (Elephant task)
- Measure progress against the plan.

Benefits of planning

- Helps us to prepare.
- Organises time.
- Sets direction.
- Monitor how we have improved.
- Can plan to spend more time customer facing – 'doing the right things.
- Simplest way to earn more, spend more time with people who buy!

Planning - Time logs

- Why make a time log? To assess how we really spend our time.
- How can we do things differently and save time and make improvements?

Financial planning

- Calculate your potential earnings.
- What activities do we earn money from doing?
- How can we do more of the things we earn money for?
- What are the new potential earnings?
- How can we ensure we achieve higher earnings?

SMART Objectives

- Specific
- Measurable
- Ambitious
- Realistic
- Time bound

Measure progress

- Monitor progress against the plan.
- Adapt plan to shifting business landscapes.
- Self-competence assessment. Identify training needs.
- Develop training solutions.
- Ask for help.
- GROWTH Model coaching
- Tracking ($Y = f x$)

Planning – Other tools

Tools that can leverage planning

- Prince2 – Projects IN Controlled Environments
- Kaizen – Continuous improvement
- Kanban – Process of systemised work
- 7 wastes - Waiting, Overproduction, Transportation, Inappropriate processing, Excessive inventory, Unnecessary motion, Defects
- 6 Sigma – Eliminates Defects
- 5's – Sort, Set in order, Shine, Standardise, Sustain

Planning – Key Benefits

- Sets direction
- Everyone knows how & where they fit in
- Everyone knows their role
- Increases the chances of success
- Recognise deviances from the plan
- Can make timely corrections to stay on course
- Arrive on schedule at the destination

Planning & The entrepreneur

- Plans can be formal or informal
- Formal plans are necessary for external partners
- Informal plans are ok for internal activities
- However, for leverage & scale it is more practical to have a formal written document
- **Think Big! Unbounded beliefs!**
- **Am I thinking BIG enough? Don't be limited by negative thinking.**

Action

After planning we are ready to take some action.

Action	
Awareness	Being conscious of unfolding events and perceived consequences
Acknowledgement	Recognise the importance, quality or existence of something
Attention	Hyper-focus on one thing and ignoring irrelevant distractions
Sales Process	Highly trained and focused on professional selling
Networking	View organisations as networks not hierarchal
Rapport	Ability to recognise common ground and build trust
Training	Practice strategy until we can't get it wrong
7 Magic Questions	A structured number of sales questions that achieve results
Sales Contract	Agreeing to a negotiated set of deliverables
Advertising	The focused use of media to generate promotional awareness
Sales Presentations	Eyeball to eyeball deal busting activity that generates productivity and profit margin
Focus Efforts	Achieving more through less effort or resources means leverage
Customer Profiles	Every customer has a different profile, different motives and different expectations
Body Language	Recognising nonverbal clues helps focus on desired outcomes
Performance Management	Focus on what can be achieved, what is realistically achievable, the expected standard and the unacceptable results
Walk the Talk	Believe in the vision, spread the message and recruit like-minded people
Service	Focus on delivering impeccable customer service that builds reputation

Action – Attention

Obtaining the customer's Attention:

Hyper-focus on one thing and ignoring irrelevant distractions

- Company – Advertising & Marketing strategies
- Press
- Radio
- Television
- Internet – Social networks
- Reputation
- Personal Selling

Action – Acknowledgement

- To recognise the importance, quality or existence of something

Why we acknowledge customers:

- People like to be engaged in conversations
- The worse thing we can do is ignore our customers

How to acknowledge customers:

- Consider the type of industry environment where we meet our customers
- Develop effective means of engaging customers through acknowledgement

Action – Awareness

Awareness: Being conscious of unfolding events and perceived consequences

- Ensure the customer is aware you are there to help
- Be visible, people, products, buildings
- Be approachable
- Be ready to assist and answer questions
- Be aware of other customers (who may want to buy)

Action – Meeting & Greeting

- Establish communication channels.
- Put the customer at ease.
- Establish rapport.

Action – First impressions:

- Importance of first impressions.
- How to create a good first impression.
- What to do if the customer does not relate to you or your style.
- Building rapport.
- Building trust
- Advertising
- Networking

Action – Breaking the ice:

- Ice breakers.
- Non sales questions
- Building rapport.
- Building trust
- Advertising
- Networking

Action – Building rapport & Trust

Ability to recognise common ground and build trust

- Why Build Rapport – customer will begin to like you
- How to build Rapport – look for common ground
- Use non-sales questions that help to build a picture of the customer's behavioural patterns.

Building trust:

- Build rapport
- Establish a likeable relationship
- Customer will begin to trust you and if he trusts you, he will buy from you

Action – Networking:

View organisations as networks not hierarchal (or competition)

- When we join a network, we enter a psychological contract for the greater good of the network. This means we may or may not receive a benefit from networking activities however, as a whole, the network will win every time there is growth amongst the network members.
- Being part of a network has many benefits:
- Increase your customer base
- Increase future opportunities
- Increase reputation, credibility and goodwill
- Provide reciprocal benefits to network members

Action – Sales strategy

High-level considerations and decisions as to how we will compete

- The products we will offer
- The customers we will target
- The marketing we will adopt
- The locations we will sell from
- The ambiance, atmosphere and environment
- The image we will portray
- The reputation we will build and protect

Action – Sales pitch

Sales presentation: A practiced sequence of information, advice and questions

Consider everything that must be included in your sales presentation eg:

- Planning what may and may not happen and controls
- Building rapport & trust, the type of customer we attract
- Tell them why we are great, what we sell, generate interest
- The questions we may ask to establish problems and solutions
- The product features and benefits and advantages for the customer
- How we may seal the relationship with win win outcomes (sales)
- Structure in place to debrief sales presentations and improve

Action – Sales contract

Sales contract: Agreeing to a negotiated set of deliverables
The paperwork must be 'watertight', check that standard forms meet the company requirements, train staff to complete accurately, check the contracts twice!

- Contact Details
- What the parties have agreed to
- The delivery date
- The payment
- Signatures

Action – 7 magic questions

7 magic questions:

A structured number of sales questions that achieve results
- Using questions to improve conversion ratio
- Determine the 7 most important sales questions
- Without exception these 7 questions must be asked to every customer

Action – Hyper-selling

Focus efforts / Hyper-selling: Achieving more through less effort or resources means leverage

- Total focus on sales, sales teams and customer wants & needs
- Focus on the competition and what we can do to win market share

Strategies may include:
- Sales training
- Differentiation
- Price matching
- Quality

Action – Customer profiles

Customer profiles: Every customer has a different profile, different motives and different expectations

- Consider the different types of customer profiles we attract:
- Leader / Driver / Achiever type
- Manager / Expressive / Social type
- Inventor / Analytical, Amiable/ Security type
- Consider how we may adapt our style for each customer type

Action – Body language

Body language: Recognising non-verbal clues will help focus on desired outcomes

- Facial gestures
- Body posture, arms & legs
- Personal space
- Eye contact
- Social touching
- Handshakes
- Parting

Action – Performance Management

Performance Management:

- Focus on what can be achieved, what is realistically achievable, the expected standard and the unacceptable results
- Qualitative & quantifiable objectives
- SMART objectives
- Targets
- Break even measurements (Favourable & unfavourable results identified)

Action – Performance management

Performance management:

- Start with the best outcome 1
- Adjust sails contingency A
- Adjust sails contingency B
- Adjust sails contingency C
- Set Direction
- Monitor
- Review
- Correct

Action – Walk the talk

Walk the talk:

Believe in the vision, spread the message, and recruit like-minded people

- Set vision
- Agree goal, targets
- Align values
- Everyone behind the plan
- Aim to win
- Never falter
- Share successes

Action – Service

Service: Focus on delivering impeccable customer service that builds reputation

- The standards we expect to achieve
- The standards our customers expect
- Mandatory features and benefits (that the customer expects to be there)
- What we do to ensure everything runs smoothly
- What we will do when things go downhill!
- How we will retain our customers for the long term (Raving fans)

Action – Key Benefits

- Opportunity to make a great first impression.
- Improve professional appearance of the organisation
- Increase the opportunity of matching the problem to the solution
- Increase chances of customers buying from us
- Gaining Commitment from the Customer to Buy from YOU!
- Repeat sales
- Referrals & Recommendations

Action & The Entrepreneur

Actions we must take to succeed:

- Focus on structured action builds a platform for success
- Common actions provide leverage
- Aim to systemise the key money-making activities
- Do more of the money-making activities to achieve leverage of activities
- Leverage means scale opportunity
- This increases income and profit margin

Interest, Ingenuity, Intention

We have identified solutions to problems and identified our goals. The next logical step is to tell the world about our products and services.

PAIDBACK – Intention, Ingenuity & Interest

Intention	Ingenuity	Interest
Business Case	USP	Benefit Statement
Why we are in Business	Why we are better than the competition	Why you should buy from us

Intention

The business case is the reason we are in business. We must inform our potential customers of our intention to sell.

Ingenuity – USP

Tell them how good we are and why we intend to capture market share. (USP - Unique Selling Proposition).

Interest - Benefit statement

Tell them how good we are and why they should buy from us, this is known as the 'benefit statement'!

Desire

Desire is an important part of PAIDBACK, we need customers to buy our products and they will only purchase if we can stimulate a desire to own the goods and part with their hard earned cash.

Problems – Identify wants and needs
Issues – what issues are causing our customer's pain?
Constraints – What problems are preventing our customer's pleasure?
Objections – Handle customer questions
Questioning skills – Use open and closed questions and the 'Tell Me Technique'
Listening skills – Demonstrate Active Listening
Price / cost – Problems with discounts and effect on margin
Solutions – The solution must meet the customer's wants and needs

Benefits & Features

Features Benefits & Advantages

Customers don't buy pieces of wood, metal and foam. They buy what the product will do for them they buy features, benefits and advantages

Therefore, we must understand features benefits and advantages, as these are a key part of an entrepreneur's strategy. Great salespeople understand how they must match the product features and benefits to the customers wants and needs and provide the advantages of owning the product over the retaining of the money (the price). Customers will buy when the features, benefits and advantages outweigh the purchase price.

Therefore, entrepreneurs must learn how to identify features, benefits and advantages and to recognise how to identify and fulfill customers wants and needs.

Complexity: Features & Benefits

Understanding features and benefits helps us to sell products but knowing about advantages helps us close deals. So, what's the difference?

Terms vary:

There are many different ways of dealing with features and benefits. Here, for simplicity, we will use features, benefits & advantages. Other terms include attribute and function. It's not unusual to find that one person's benefit is another's advantage! However, what's important is that features are related to the customer's wants and needs. We can only do this by understanding our customer's problem and matching the features that provide solutions (benefits) and moves the customer to a better position (advantages).

Feature: What it is!

The product features are the technical facts about the product or service. Features include colour, dimensions, weight and functions etc. features are normally found in product data sheets & are often seen in advertisements. Features raise interest, demonstrates product knowledge and talking about features helps to break the ice with customers, build trust and rapport.

Technically minded customers may have a checklist of features required, other customers may be keen to learn about the product they are searching for.

Features however, are not likely to close a sale but will help build trusting relations.

Benefits: What it does.

The benefits are the reason a customer may want to buy your products or services. We should build features and benefits into the sales presentation so that the conversation flows naturally from the early stages.

We should try to demonstrate the features and benefits that the customers want and need and uncover some they hadn't thought of.

Some salespeople ask 'so what' after they've made a statement which helps to find the end rather than the means. Focus on finding benefits for every feature. This will provide new ways of sales negotiation.

Advantages

Advantages: What it does for you

Customers will only buy when the advantages of owning the product or receiving the service are worth more than keeping their money. This is the discerning factor in entrepreneurship. We must find ways of presenting advantages to customers, so they feel justified in parting with their hard-earned cash.

By focusing on the wants and needs already uncovered we can provide specific solutions to the customers identified problems. When we follow this type of process this builds trust and confidence in the organisation and the next logical step is commitment to purchase.

The words features, benefits and advantages are used throughout the business process and there's no reason why we can't use these terms at every level of business negotiations.

Features, benefits and advantages and knowing the difference will help you improve professionalism and increase sales.

Having determined the customer's problems and their wants and needs we must provide a product that has the features, benefits and advantages that fulfill the customer's wants and needs.

Connection, Cheque & Check

Connection is about building a relationship with someone. We must assume that when we meet someone for the first time, we are unconnected, there are no positives or negatives. In a trusting relationship we would expect each party to have many positive experiences of each other and to be open and transparent to each other's wants and needs.

There also appears to be a hierarchy of trust, from known to like to trust. People must 'know' you first. Are you smart and presentable, happy or sad, interested in me, or your surroundings and have you chosen your greeting wisely? People like or dislike other people in a matter of a split second, we make instant decisions about people we meet based on our first impressions, get it wrong and it's a long road back, a near impossible one. Once we like each other the conversation is easier, we can build rapport, identify common interests and start to trust each other to do what they say they can.

Cheque is how we get paid, so no matter how crude it may seem or how alien it is for you to ask for money, if you don't your business will die, no cash flow means death. So, "Ask For The Order".

Check the fine details of the actions you will take to satisfy your customers. I used to say that we haven't got time to check it once, but we always have time to check it twice! This way we will protect the business we worked so hard to achieve, we will ensure our processes can deliver the order, we will ensure we get paid, we will satisfy our customer and build our reputation, credibility and our business.

Connection

Trust
Reciprocal - Win Win
Friendships
Relationships
Network expansion
Referrals
Repeat business
Singing waving fans – Our customers are satisfied enough to tell the world

AAA – Another Alternative Agreement:

When we can't agree on the current proposals, think about an alternative that can fulfill the customer's wants and needs. Even if we just agree to think about the solution for a few days.

Another Alternative Agreement - AAA	
Trust	Takes years to build and can be lost in seconds
Win Win	There's no losers in our negotiations only reciprocal trusting relationships and long term future business
Friendships	Start here
Singing Waving Fans	Ultimate objective, happy customers who tell the world
Relationships	We must build long term relations
Network Expansion	Spread the word, everything is a 'Value Network' - customers, suppliers, employees
Referrals	Ask for referrals to demonstrate trust and commitment
Repeat Business	We must give everyone a reason to come back to us

Closing questions – We must get commitment to buy and maintain relations.

Trust

When a customer or client likes us, they will trust us and only when they believe they will receive value for their money, and we will deliver in the agreement will they buy from us.

Win & Win

If we are to increase our sales, we need our customers to enter a reciprocal agreement where both parties to the contract receive some mutual benefit from the relationship

Friendships

The best relationships are arguably friendships. Based on a reciprocal trust the conversation between friends is easy

Relationships

Relationships are hard to build but easy to lose

Network expansion

The only way we can expand our networks is through focus on increasing the number of relations

Referrals

When people have a great service or experience from our people, they are highly likely to refer business to us, (free)

Repeat business

When people have a problem free experience with our people, they are more likely to visit us again

Singing customers and waving fans – who tell the world about your business

Even when things go wrong, put it right, provide great products, services and care and your customers will still support you

Closing questions

The only way to move forward is by asking a closing question. Eg Are you happy for us to do this for you? Seal the relationship you have just made with a decision for firm action at the agreed price. You must find a way to connect and ASK FOR THE ORDER.

Key benefits of a strategy to connect include:

Increase our relationships
Provide reciprocal opportunities & Aim for win win outcomes
Improve chance of referrals & repeat business
Gain a friend for life

Summary

Connection is all about network capital

However, we must ask Closing questions too

Knowledge

Definition of Knowledge:

- Bits, bytes, data, information, know-how, facts, and skills acquired through experience, training or education, the theoretical or practical understanding of a subject.

Learning Organisation:

A learning organisation is capable of continual regeneration from the variety of knowledge, experience and skills of individuals through a culture that encourages mutual questioning and challenge around a shared purpose or vision

Knowledge Planning	
Knowledge Identify	Systems in place to identify gaps
Knowledge Capture & Storage	Record information and retain
Knowledge Make re-usable	Transfer data into knowledge
Knowledge Make accessible	Provides scale, leverage and power

- Identify - Observe workers and identify work processes
- Capture - Map work processes
- Store - Work processes must be stored for future reference and amortisation
- Make reusable - Store in a format that can be reused for future projects, by workers, or for buy out
- Make accessible - Knowledge can be stored and made accessible through for example, standards of performance.

Learn From Experience:

- Good and bad experiences provide knowledge and learning.
- Relate experiences from inside the business and outside the business.
- Relate academic teachings to the workplace.
- Experiences are interpreted differently by different people
- Learning From Mistakes is an Expensive Way to Learn

Best people are Knowledge workers:

- Skilled workers
- Trained employees
- Industry Experience
- Leadership Experience
- Innovators
- Managers
- Relevant education degrees, PhD's
- Must be enthusiastic, Positive mental attitude!

Knowledge Sources

- Trade Publications.
- Company Training Materials.
- Supplier Information.
- Salespeople.
- Competitors.
- Each Other.
- Customers.
- Personal Action Plan.

Knowledge Benefits

- Knowledge is power (when it is shared)
- Identifies Opportunity
- Able to compete
- Enables Innovation, Change, Survival

The Ingredients of Entrepreneur as Manager

Entrepreneur as Manager

How we manage the venture rewards

Manages Value

The dominant role of Entrepreneur Manager is to protect venture rewards
Secondary Roles as Entrepreneur Manager/Inventor is to spot opportunities
Secondary Roles as Entrepreneur Manager/Leader is to improve performance

Manager Role & Tasks

The entrepreneur as manager manages the rewards of the business venture and protects the business from loss of value. Rewards from the venture include both financial assets and non-financial assets. All tangible assets include cash, wages, property, plant and machinery. Intangible or non-financial assets are more difficult to identify and quantify, nevertheless, the manager must identify intangible assets, measure them and protect them from loss of value. Intangible assets will include knowledge, processes, know-how, tricks of the trade, training and training partners, key workers, health & safety, security, time etc. The best protection is to convert intangible assets to tangible assets through transparency. For example, identify which employees are key workers and detail their work processes then protects the venture from loss of key workers knowledge with appropriate contractual arrangements.

Entrepreneur Managers Protect

What's the role of an entrepreneur manager?

Our entrepreneur manager is responsible for managing the value created by the venture. The dominant role is to ensure the business does not suffer losses. Therefore, the entrepreneur as manager is also a financial controller, a HR department, an operations manager, an auditor as well as also being an inventor and a leader. The entrepreneur manager is able to efficiently manage resources in a way that exploits market knowledge to meet customer demand and protect resources against preventable economic loss. So, the entrepreneur manager protects value. This can also include exploiting opportunity and leveraging resources for example investing money in new ventures or funds and selling employee expertise to competitors. The primary aim of the manager is to protect wealth, but this can include generating wealth to. As we can see from the definition below the entrepreneur manager has unlimited boundaries.

Protect definition: 'to defend our venture, financial and Resource Value resources, workforce, customers, suppliers, partners and other stakeholders from loss, attack, insult or injury'.

Value Management

Being successful is as much about value management as profit generation! The secret is to have a simple system that becomes habitual and is used daily. Protecting rewards is an essential component of entrepreneurship and this includes financial, other tangible and intangible rewards.

Protecting our hard-earned efforts is not just about cash but everything we have built through this venture sometimes known as Network Value and includes how we value goodwill and our reporting strategies. It's all about relationships, reputation, credibility and poor value management, poor customer service, poor quality control and poor HR strategies are good examples of how businesses can suffer losses either losses of customers, loss of goodwill, loss of employees and loss of profits.

Value-management is the protection of the relations and networks we have created through our ventures. Through the protection of our relationships and networks with employees, customers, partners, suppliers and all other stakeholders we can grow our credibility and reputation as a good business to do business with. Entrepreneur manages are averse to loss and therefore a good place to start with value management is to assess the tangible assets and intangible assets that we need to protect.

The PROTECT Model	
Protect	Definition: To defend our venture, financial and intellectual capital resources, workforce, customers, suppliers, partners and other stakeholders from loss, attack, insult or injury.
Process	Recipes for success, products, patents, copyright, knowledge, trade secrets, networks, relationships, strategies and contingencies. Structural Capital.
Risk Reporting Relations	Identify Risk Report on both tangibles and intangibles to maintain, develop and defend reputation and strengthen networks and create value through goodwill. Through every growth activity the recording of inputs both tangible and intangible provides accurate data used to establish true costs of projects and value goodwill. Build reputation and credibility by identifying and removing risks and a reporting strategy of full transparency. Value management – how we value, control, report and protect our reputation with our stakeholders including our people, customers, suppliers etc. Relational Capital.
Operations	Property, premises, machinery, tools, production, supply chain, vehicles and insurance.
Tactics	Measuring Risk and Uncertainty to maximise gains and minimise loss. Attitude to risk (averse / acceptance), risk tolerance, methods, standards, partners, trainers, training, meetings, communication, competition, knowledge. Tactical objectives and the means of achievement = competitive advantage
Employees	Wages, rewards, loyalty, pensions, commission, contracts, health & safety, risk assessments, HR policies, SOP, data protection, unions, retention, key workers, succession, culture, training, promotions, personal data, identity. Human Capital.
Capital	Generation, leverage, security, investment, tax reliefs and allowances, liabilities, schemes, interest free loans. Stock, losses, compensation, legal costs, utilities, fraud, audit systems. Networks – protect our hard-earned efforts, not just cash but everything we have built through this venture = Relational Capital
Time	Management, leverage and waste Business life cycle Work / life balance Succession planning, exit strategy

PROTECT

Process
Risk, Reporting & Relations
Operations
Tactics
Employees
Cash (Not just cash)
Time

The PROTECT mnemonic is a tool for:

Business survival
Value management
Relation management

PROTECT is a system for managing value through relational strategies. This is how we leverage network capital, the relations, networks and rewards of the business venture.

PROTECT provides a framework to protect the rewards from the business including trade secrets, people, key workers and time etc, this list is not exhaustive.

Success is difficult to achieve but survival can be just as tough, having strategies to manage business rewards can raise the probability of business survival. PROTECT is a framework that helps focus our minds on business survival, protecting & leveraging venture rewards and

Process

We might start with the way in which we actually do business such as process, systems that comprise the structure of the business. Things we might want to protect from our competitors may include recipes for success, our products, patents, copyright, company knowledge, trade secrets, networks, relationships, strategies, and contingencies.

Most businesses have less than 100 processes. Processes enable businesses to leverage resources and grow exponentially. Processes enable us to train new people to standard and when people know where the business is going our minds focus on achieving these goals and find breakthrough ways of achievement. Processes provide a means to measure the things we do or don't do that can impact our profits and costs and are therefore a measure of efficiency and value-delivery. Processes should be mapped as we can make money from knowledge and develop the rules that should be obeyed. Start with the way in which we actually do business such as process, systems that comprise the structure of the business. Things we might want to protect from our competitors may include recipes for success, our products, patents, copyright, company knowledge, trade secrets, networks, relationships, strategies, and contingencies.

Patents

A patent is a government grant to a creator of an invention providing the sole right to make use and sell that invention for a period of time. Patents are a cost to a business as they have to be obtained and maintained. However, they provide an opportunity for market exclusivity for a period of time. The drawback is the patent information is made public allowing competitors to advance on your market. Bill Gates is quoted about patents having the 'shelf life of a banana', much better to have trade secrets.

Patents may also interfere with the company mission; Tesla Motors released all its patents to advance its mission through providing competitors with green technology contained in its patents.

Copyright ©

Copyright is a legal right granted to an author, playwright, publisher or distributor for the exclusive production, publication, distribution and sale of literary, musical, dramatic or artistic works. Copyright means due credit and compensation for the duration of the author's life plus 50 years but there are exceptions for fair use. Plagiarism is unethical and unprofessional but not an offence and does not apply to factual information.

Products

Products are a result of a good idea created by a process of manufacture that satisfy a want or need. Products have both tangible and intangible attributes such as features, benefits and advantages that a buyer wants or needs, and a seller can exploit for a profit. For example, the seller of a razor not only offers for sale the physical product but also the benefit that the consumer will be improving their appearance as well.

Products allow other entrepreneurs to identify new markets and provide direct and indirect complementary products and services. For example, a car provides the opportunity to supply services and parts such as tyres, brake pads, exhausts, wax polish, oil, fuel, roads, air fresheners, car mats etc.

Policies & Procedures

Policies and procedures are an organisational rulebook, formally accepted by the employer and employees and usually published in a form of handbook, such as HR Policies, Health & Safety Policies. Entrepreneurs in start-up mode are without a guide to achieve their long-term goals, this is where policies and procedures can help to keep the business on track as these allow processes to be followed that leverage resources. This means everyone in the organisation, no matter where in the world will follow the same systems to achieve organisational goals. Either write your own policies and procedures, copy procedures from many templates available or instruct an expert company to map your processes and generate policies and procedures for you (expensive route).

Strategies

The future achievement of the organisational goals relies on a method or plan more formally known as a strategy. A strategy is the direction of the company, it provides the company aims, what we are trying to achieve and how we will achieve these aims.

Recipes for Success

A recipe for success is a procedure for accomplishing something such as a set of directions, a list of ingredients, a formula, a means of production. Cross reference recipes for success v recipe for disaster.

Know-how

Know-how is a term for something that is often difficult to write down or formalise in a way that can be transferred to another person. It is referred to as tacit knowledge (in the heads of people) rather than explicit knowledge (formalised in policies and procedures). Know-how examples include, expert skill, common knowledge, industry information and techniques.

Trade Secrets

A trade secret is knowledge of a commercial method for achieving something that is not generally known or easily ascertainable by others such as competitors. A trade secret normally provides a method of competitive advantage in entrepreneurial environments that results in an economic profit. Courts will normally enforce the threatened disclosure of trade secrets by former employees and prudent employers will contract employees to confidentially agreements. Trade secrets can include the method for producing something, intellectual property or customer lists and the definition of trade secrets is considered non-exhaustive.

Networks

Networks are made up of communities where individual relationships are built on reciprocal trust that provides win win outcomes. However, networks must be viewed for the greater good of providing options and opportunities for the network rather than for the individuals that comprise the network. For example, the network may grow, and some people will benefit but others may not benefit, however the network will always benefit.

Structural Capital

Everything left in the building when the gates are locked. Capital suggests the need to measure this resource.

Contingencies

In a situation where the result is unknown or unpredictable a possible event must be prepared for. This preparation is known as a contingency plan.

Licensing Agreement

Other people will pay you for your ideas and this allows you to leverage your knowledge. A licensing agreement is a contract allowing a licensee to use your intellectual property under strict terms. Manufacturers use these but so do franchisors.

Misappropriation

Dishonestly appropriating someone else's intellectual property or trade secrets can lead to expensive litigation.

Risk Reporting & Relations

Risk

Taking risks through entrepreneurial activities is the only way to grow, as opposed to holding on to safety and the status quo is a sure way to die. Static efficiency is a comfort zone and rarely provides growth whereas dynamic efficiency and entrepreneur action drive the entrepreneur ingredient of creative destruction. Risks are identified and therefore not gambling with uncertainty.

Reduce uncertainty

When we measure risks, we identify them and make the risk more transparent. This makes an uncertain future a little more certain.

Risk attitude (averse/accept)

Attitude to risk may depend on a particular industry, private ambulance services or smartphone companies may have very different approaches, but it's all relative to the industry and not the external environment. The extremes of risk attitude are either risk averse or risk acceptance. However, taking risks or not taking risks can also be risky. A more prudent approach may be somewhere in the middle, a balanced approach to risk management.

Risk tolerance is an important component in investing. An individual should have a realistic understanding of his or her ability and willingness to stomach large swings in the value of his or her investments. Investors who take on too much risk may panic and sell at the wrong time.

Risk tolerance is a more specific measure of the degree of uncertainty that an investor is willing to accept in respect of negative changes to its business or assets, as opposed to risk appetite being a broad-based level. (Generic)
Tolerance is the acceptable level of deviation relative to the achievement of objectives. In setting specific risk tolerances, management considers the relative importance of related objectives and aligns risk tolerances with its risk appetite.
The business must protect against risk outside what is acceptable or tolerated.

Measure risk

To protect against risk a measure is a good place to start. Also, having a strategy in place to measure risks and provide opportunity enables us to correct unfavourable deviances. Monitor the strategy and take corrective action, whether this is people, product or services, tangibles or intangibles.

Reporting

Since we are trying to build our business, our reputation and goodwill is important so that we become credible, and our customers want to do business with us over and over again. Therefore, it is very advantageous to report on tangible and intangible assets in a way that builds reputation and credibility. Being a transparent business helps attract customers and helps maintain, develop and defend reputation but also strengthen networks and create value through goodwill. Through every growth activity the recording of inputs both tangible and intangible provides accurate data we can use to report and establish true costs of projects and value goodwill.

Tangible Assets

Tangible assets or physical assets are easily accounted for and include both fixed assets such as property, land, buildings, tools, plant and machinery and current assets such as inventory.

Intangible Assets

Intangible assets or non-financial assets are more difficult to measure and account for. Intangible assets include patents, trademarks, copyrights, and goodwill and brand recognition.

True costs of projects (Measuring intangibles too)

Record tangible inputs such as Money and other tangible resources
Record intangible inputs such as people, ideas etc and time

Account for everything that contributes to the development and completion of projects. Include all inputs whether these are tangible or intangible as the cost of developing a process, procedure, product or strategy all contribute to the goodwill of the company which needs to be valued at some point.

Reporting on Opportunity - Create / retain value

1. Managers must retain the value created in the business venture
2. Managers must also understand the concept of opportunity recognition and opportunity creation, i.e., in the course of managing the value created is there an opportunity to exploit or alternatively can we invest resources to create an opportunity. Managers, therefore, wear a coordinator's hat and ORGANISE.

Relations

Networks are all about building relationships and the deeper the trust the more valuable our relationships become. The same rule applies in personal relationships and business relationships. Family, friends, mates, pals, butty, buddies, fans, customers or clients what's yours called. What's the degree of trust between you and those who buy from you? Looking after these people in whom you have invested both time and money and are the purpose of your existence is key to your survival. Customers and customer lists are your long-term assets and provide value or goodwill in your business and must be looked after if your business is to survive and grow. No matter what business you're in, you need customers, but every business has different types of customers.

However, customers are people, and we should start by treating people as people as we don't know if we will sell over and over again to the same person or never see them again. Irrespective of how we think or feel, a customer experience good or bad will influence whether the customer returns or not or tells others about your standard of service. Our standard of service must be of the highest professional standards at all times, or we will lose customers.

The best relationships are the ones where we trust each other to do the right thing by each other and the relationship is reciprocal. Even when we mess up, say the wrong thing or even hurt someone through thoughtlessness the relationship stays strong. How can we build this in business, is it possible to build customer relationships then let them down yet still retain customer loyalty.

It's about people. People by products, brands, companies but most of all they buy people. Whether this is the polite and courteous assistant in the local pound store or the CEO of an airline or Multi-national, when we have a recipe for success both internally and externally it's the people who deliver the service that makes the difference. But it's not just about service delivery it's more about the relationships that are being built because people are being, well, just people. Friendly, polite and knowledgeable and doing what you say you will do is all people expect. Build great relationships to a level of high trust and even though things may go wrong in the morning there is understanding and an expectation that the high trusting relationship is a platform for remedies. Families do this, so do supermarkets, phone companies and car manufacturers and many retailers.

I found there are four customer relational types:

Do your job - Professional service and nothing else.
Lovers not fighters - Trusting relationships
CRM - Service with a smile
Gold Standard - Aim for long lasting professional service and trusting relationships.

CRT - Customer Relational Types	
CRM Those who want service with a smile	**Gold Standard** Those who want long lasting professional service and trusting relationships
Do your job Those who want professional service and nothing else.	**Lovers not fighters** Those who want trusting relationships

Measuring Service, Recognising Relations and How to Handle:

What do these relationships tell us about our customers and our service levels?

Do your job – Passing Acquaintance

Customers who want professional service and nothing else. These people will make the decision to purchase. They don't believe you and they know what they are looking for. They believe their standards are higher than yours. They want the best and expect you to provide it. They won't give you anything but the price, may want discount too. Give advice and options and let them make their own decisions.

Lovers not fighters - Besties

Customers who want trusting relationships. These customers want to avoid trouble and value friendships. They believe that friends will look after their relationships. Therefore, they build friendships and hopefully this means a safe purchase. They will give you their loyalty and in return they expect the product quality to reflect the price paid. Get on their side and don't let them down.

CRM – Mates with Benefits

Customers who want service with a smile. This is the general expectation of most retailers and their customers. Retailers understand a certain standard of service must be provided to entice customers to buy. The retailer views this service as a cost and minimizes training and service levels in line with profits. Customers expect a mandatory level of service, the things they would expect to be there for the type of store and type of product on offer. These customers are often disappointed that the smile hides a façade when things go wrong.

Gold Standard – Non-intimate Family

Some people want long lasting professional service and trusting relationships. The customer is expecting mandatory features and benefits. This may include free delivery, guarantees to put things right and compensation schemes. These customers expect to be involved with your business, will offer free advice and hope to help you raise your standards. They want you to be the best and they will only buy the best. These are customers for life. They buy quality and will only be associated with top quality retailers. Build trust, offer support, focus on a high level of engagement and when things go wrong, be there, take fast action.

The level of engagement with your customers may depend on the type of company and industry your product supports. Arguably, for cost driven companies the level of service may be affected relatively. However, in reality customer service costs nothing and the dividends are tenfold, every customer has a right to be provided with exceptional professional service, looked after when things go wrong and encouraged to recommend and refer your business when they are happy with the relationship.

Do your job - Professional service and nothing else.

Passing Acquaintance. We may never see these customers again. Unscrupulous retailers may see this as a one off sale and offer a professional service that offers value for price premiums that creates high margins knowing that the customer will never return anyway. However, there is an opportunity to get this customer onside and provide a level of service that is above what they expect, just one tweet of happiness may be enough to secure a future sale from a passing acquaintance relationship.

Lovers not fighters - Trusting relationships

Besties. Business is all about people. When people like us they will trust us, and they will buy from us. They will pay the price and have low expectations of the quality and service. They may never complain to you when things go wrong. However, let these people down and the whole world will know about it as they want the whole world to be their besties too.

CRM - Service with a smile
(Mates with benefits) Customers expect you to provide a great service and do something a little bit special for them to cement the relationship, they also expect you to be on their side when things go wrong, and the service department is dragging their heels with your complaint. Keeping the customer and the sales means looking after the relationship too and may cost you money in compensation.

Gold Standard – (Long lasting professional service and trusting relationships)

Non-intimate Families. We want our families to be protected from harm, to enjoy their days and be worry free. When things go wrong, we want to be able to analyse the issues, understand the problems, offer support, take away the pain and move to a more pleasurable state. Here the relationship is of power and interest. The power being all with the business in most cases and interest in providing a solution to the problem shared. The environment is often a parent to child situation and raising the level to an adult-to-adult conversation is often key to resolving the issues and maintaining the relationship. Great businesses want to provide products and services to meet their customer's wants and needs. They want their customers to buy from them over and over again and to recommend and refer the relationship to their friends. The aim must be to provide quality, worry free products and services that perform as we say they will and to provide consistent high levels of support and concern when things go wrong. The relationship is of the highest importance, so are reputation and trust.

Social Speak

Take away the people and focus on the problem. Everything your company does builds or destroys your reputation and credibility. Therefore, we must focus on building a positive relationship with our customers through every interaction, even when we are wrong or perceived to be wrong. This is always a marketing opportunity to build our credibility. Don't leave this opportunity to IT people either, bring in sales teams and psychologists to monitor and advise on social media content or you could be missing a trick to build the love and make sure we solve the problem.

The Customer's Always Right

Take away the problem and focus on the people. Happy customers tell 2 people, unhappy customers tell the whole world. Even when things go wrong people are still people. Only focusing on the problem demonstrates a disregard for why we are in business, people are the reason why we arrived at this point. Therefore, we must up our game and deal with the people issues that are hardest. Emotionally charged people can do our business substantial harm when they take to social media sites to vent their discontent and companies pay CRM specialists to trawl the internet for opportunities to put things right for their customers that complain online. Reputations and trusting relationships can be destroyed in a moment when things go wrong therefore, switched on businesses manage the problem, the people and the vehicle for spreading the message.

Network Management

The key point in network management is the building of quality trusting relationships. Building trusting relationships enhances brand reputation and the credibility of the organisation. Therefore, a network management strategy should focus on the building and protection of reputation above all else. This means focus on the customer's wants and needs and the delivery of our services that are designed to solve customer's problems and satisfy their wants and needs. This is what you wanted or needed, this is what we said we would provide, and this is what happened. What can we learn from this to put things right now and for our future customers?

There should be a strategy for Value-management - how we value, control, report and protect our reputation with all stakeholders including our people, customers, suppliers, etc (relational capital).

Specifically, a value-management strategy should focus on reporting tangible and Intangible assets that are a result of the venture and need protective measures to retain and create value. Everything that flows from a venture are venture rewards, this is the value created by business deliverables, organisational value requires a value management strategy

Strengthen networks

Strategy that considers the aims and objectives required to grow strong reciprocal business networks. A plan that ensures existing networks are maintained and strengthened while overall networks are grown with strong relations.

Build goodwill

Everything we do affects the perceived goodwill of the company. Goodwill comes from the very first idea, it increases and decreases in value as the company grows and matures. Goodwill valuation is the ultimate key performance indicator

Control reputation

Internal confidences will affect external relations and reputation. So, in order to control reputation, there must be strict internal control or hygiene factors that provide cultural cohesion, trust and mutuality.

Stakeholders

A stakeholder is someone who has an interest in an enterprise or project. The primary stakeholders in a typical business are its investors, employees, customers and suppliers.

Build reputation

Develop systems, processes, products or services that reflect your company mission. Whatever you do it to the standards you have set and never falter

Build credibility

Walk the talk

Maintain reputation

Develop a corporate culture that drives the reputation of the company, everyone behind the company reputation

Develop reputation

Actively market the company reputation in a transparent way

Defend reputation

Court, customer service

Operations

Operations relate to the tangible elements of the business and include property, premises, machinery, tools, plant, production and supply chain and vehicles. In most cases risk can be offset through insurance policies. The key benefits of having a risk control plan for our operations ensures we focus on controlling costs, identifying risk, developing contingencies, recognizing emerging opportunities and creating opportunities through the recognition and development of breakthrough strategies. (A breakthrough puts us into a new position that moments before we thought impossible). While managers are responsible for managing existing resources derived from the business there are always opportunities for breakthroughs.

Property & Premises

Property and premises include the land and outbuildings and everything in the buildings, these are either occupied by the business or considered as business assets. Certain risks and liabilities will result from owning property and the risk to the business must be assessed. Costs will include rates and rents but also maintenance and property valuations particularly in downturns and where there is heavy borrowing against property assets.

Most businesses will need some sort of premises or property as the business grows and entrepreneurs try to scale the business by leveraging resources. Buying property and machinery means liabilities to furnish borrowing as well as other liabilities such as for injury under health and safety legislation. These types of risks must be offset to ensure the business survives and the entrepreneurs stay clear of litigation.

When looking for business premises consider the real business requirements. Take legal advice on lease agreements and liability for repairs. Negotiate a free period for early access to prepare building for trading and a few months' rent free trading, this will help accumulate much needed cash flow and improve the chance of business survival.

Pros and Cons

Machinery reduces costs through automation and leverages processes.
Mechanics makes effective use of load and force
Systems organize resources to be more efficient

Machinery is a substantial cost to the business, ties up capital, requires loans or investment and also costs when idle, under maintenance or broken. These are all factors to consider when determining scale factors.

Tools

An item or implement used for a specific purpose. A tool can be a physical object such as hammers and chisels or a technical object such as a software programme or a sales tool. 5s philosophy can help manage tools (Sort, Set in order, Shine, Standardise, Sustain).

Means of Production

The means of production, aside from people, include all the tangible or physical elements that contribute to the manufacture of goods and services. This includes natural resources, machines, tools, offices, computers and software but also includes the means of distribution such as transport, warehouses and the internet. While the means of production and the means of distribution changes with time the concept is extremely important for wealth creation. Therefore, managing and protecting value and the means of production is an essential entrepreneurial task, breakthroughs here can provide exponential growth opportunities and save valuable financial resources.

Supply Network (Previously Supply Chain)

The networks that we build are both supply and customer networks, so start thinking of your supply chain as a supply network. Those we buy from will also buy from us and tell people about us and therefore expand our network, it's a reciprocal relationship and contributes to growth.

Supply networks are a complex supply and demand system of organisations, people, and information, tangible and intangible resources necessary for the production of products and services and the delivery from supplier to customers.

Vehicles

Used for the transport of people or goods. Vehicles are always a cost. Does the company need vehicles at all? Type, fuel, outsourcing etc

Insurance

Risk transfer mechanism that ensures full or partial compensation for specific loss or damage beyond the control of the injured party, for a specific amount over a defined period.

Insurance covers tangible losses inly and intangibles needed to rebuild the organisation after a fire such as knowledge and systems would not be covered. Therefore, to mitigate risk managers must consider the value of organisational knowledge and gather knowledge, store it and make it reusable and accessible.

Tactics

Tactics are the activities we will undertake to achieve the company aims and objectives.

Tactical considerations include maximising gains and minimising loss:

Maximise gains

A process that increases the current net value of business or shareholder capital gains, with the objective of bringing in the highest possible return. The wealth maximization strategy generally involves making sound financial investment decisions that take into consideration any risk factors that would compromise or outweigh the anticipated benefits.

Minimise loss

To minimise loss it's necessary to identify, analyse and assess risks then take steps to remove them, assume them, transfer or reduce their impact on the business.

Measures to reduce losses depend on the type of risk, severity, frequency, predictability and impact on the business.

Tactics may include strategies that manage, attitude to risk (averse or acceptance), risk tolerance, work methods, standards, partners, trainers, training, meetings, communication, competition, knowledge.

Cash Generation, leverage, security, investment, tax reliefs and allowances, liabilities, schemes, insurance, interest free loans, stock, losses, compensation, legal costs, utilities, fraud, audit systems.
Networks - protect
Examples:

Reduce risk - health and safety policies
Avoid risk - eliminate uncertainties
Prepare for risk - contingency plans
Transfer risk - insurance

Methods / standards

An established, habitual, logical, or prescribed practice or systematic process of achieving certain ends and meeting agreed standards, goal and targets with accuracy and efficiency, usually in an ordered sequence of fixed steps.

Use of knowledge

Strategies to identify, gather, store and make knowledge reusable and accessible.

Awareness of standards of performance and contracts, daily debrief, training meetings, strategy meetings, growth meetings etc

Partners

Partners include networks and relationships that drive growth and contribute to business success.

Trainers

Trainers are able to help entrepreneurs deliver on targets through meeting tactical objectives. Trainers, therefore, pose a confidence risk as they develop specialist insider knowledge about the business over and above any other partner or stakeholder.

Communication

Any entrepreneurial task or transaction that requires more than one person can only be successfully completed through communication. In fact, communicating is key to networking, delivering value and growth initiatives. The entrepreneur as manager must protect the channels of communication in order to be successful and to prevent demise.

Competition

The competition is the industry, non-industry or any business or person considered as our opposition. We are trying to establish superiority over the competition in our chosen market and must succeed to survive.

Employees

Intangible or non-financial assets are also very valuable to the business and include our employees and how we provide remuneration, rewards, loyalty, pensions, commission that help retain our valuable workforce and protect the day-to-day running of the organisation. Other ways to protect employees may include contracts, health and safety, risk assessments, HR policies, SOP, data protection, unions, retention, key workers contracts, succession, culture, training, promotions, personal data, identity protection etc.

Wages

Decide or negotiate rates and frequency of payment of wages for work completed.

Pay them on time or workers will be disgruntled and leave. Credibility will be affected as bad news spreads quickly and creditors will withdraw. Once trust is lost it will be very difficult to win back customers, workers and creditors.

Rewards

Employee rewards apart from cash. Gifts are taxable so caution here. However, internal competitions, employee of the month, Christmas parties or spontaneous celebrations are not only motivational but also important for team building.

Loyalty

Loyalty works both ways. A company that is loyal to workers will have a greater chance of having loyal workers. Treat workers more poorly than expected and they will leave, most people leave because they are unhappy with managers.

Pensions

A great way to motivate long term employee relations.

Commissions

Must be carefully thought out but a great commission scheme will motivate salespeople to perform better. Beware of loopholes where discounts are made to achieve a deal, but commissions are still claimed. This increased the cost of sales and erodes profit margin.

Promotions

From within where possible. No recruitment costs. Reduces cost of training, great for motivation and team morale.

Education

Difference between teaching and training

Degrees

Relative degrees provide up to date thinking but must be managed.

Training

Internal training helps provide direction, improve performance and create loyalty. There is nothing that training can't improve.

Master's degrees

Provide higher-level thinking.

PhD's

Helps provide internal expertise.

Contracts

Contracts are necessary to provide trust and loyalty and a legal requirement.

Health & Safety

Obligations to ensure employees, customers and visitors etc are safe and your actions or inactions do not cause harm. Breach of health and safety rules will mean heavy fines, loss of credibility with employees, partners and poor reputation. It's more cost effective to have policies and procedures than not.

Risk assessments

Make sure health and safety obligations are documented and recorded. Every process must have a safe system of working and a risk assessment. Accidents must be recorded, and some are reportable to the HSE.

HR Policies

Legal obligations protect employees and company. Best approach is to find ways to make obligations under mutual contracts a motivational factor. However, expect trouble.

Standards of performance

Workers must be made aware of what is expected of them and the standards of work they must achieve so the company objectives are achieved.

Personal data

Must be kept confidential.

Data protection / identity fraud

Breach of security can have devastating consequences.

Staff retention

Cut costs and improve performance through staff retention strategies.

Key workers / skills

Key workers provide direction and help establish core competencies that drive the business. Identify key workers and the skills they have that help drive performance and develop strategies to retain the best and key workers. We should consider key worker contracts and confidential agreements.

Succession

Promote from within where possible. Consider future management buyouts, sale, takeover or acquisitions.

Culture

Company culture must support the vision. When we hear talk about culture often people are trying to define what it is. More importantly we should be asking is our culture supporting our initiatives, if not can we change the culture or change the initiative?

Culture is difficult to define. For most organisation's it's the way we do things around here, this starts on day one and stories of how the venture entrepreneurs started the business quickly become ingrained and passed down to new employees.

Culture starts at the beginning with those at the top. It's simple,

Having founding principles helps to guide culture and provides focus of what the company is about. However, most companies grow organically and setting preconceived rules is extremely difficult.

Treat people as people.
Allow people to make mistakes.
Give 100% best advice, even when it costs the contract!
Keep it simple stupid.
De-brief daily.
Challenge the status quo.
Do it once check it twice.

Culture includes everything about your business and can help retain employees, gain new business but it must be positively communicated.

Culture is what your business is about and is probably the most important part of your company.

Make A Choice

The ability to set long term goals and to see them through comes easy for some people but others will struggle with this. Nurturing entrepreneurs from a young age can introduce entrepreneurial skills, particularly the ability to focus on long-term goals and help develop the ability to put off early results in place of more gratifying rewards. Rather than focus on being weak it is very important for young people to develop entrepreneur skills in nurturing environments with lots of positive influences. Show young people that there is always a way if we look around us, focus on goals and stick with them. We should be concerned with what we can achieve instead of comparing ourselves against others but appreciate the contribution that others can make to our venture. Don't give up hope the alternatives are never really a good option.

Stress is fine and natural. Distress is a problem. (Tips)

People people should be in people jobs.
Task people should be employed in task orientated jobs.
Task people who are in people jobs or people people who are in task jobs may find these roles stressful. Acting out of character is called 'travelling' we can do this for a while but then we become stressed, distressed and head for a nervous breakdown.

Make sure we appoint the right people for the roles to benefit both the business and the people.

Capital (Not Just Cash)

Capital, not just cash, everything that flows from the venture are venture rewards, has value and must be protected from erosion and exploited where possible.

Cash (not just cash, includes Network Capital) means all the venture rewards from our hard-earned efforts and the risks we have taken. Include here relationships, networks, customer lists, supplier lists, price lists, and agreed cost of supplies.

Cash Generation, identify income streams, leverage, security, investment, tax reliefs and allowances, liabilities, schemes, insurance, interest free loans.   Stock, losses, compensation, legal costs, utilities, fraud, audit systems. Networks - protect

Cash flow

Cash flow is the business lifeblood! Without cash flow we can't pay anyone. A cash flow forecast is an essential business tool that helps a business predict how much cash is needed to run the business and how much cash will actually be available at a given time. Having a detailed and accurate cash flow forecast can help prevent cash flow issues and may even save your business from impending doom! Having an accurate cash flow forecast should be a habitual procedure and especially in a downturn.

A cash flow forecast reduces the risk of sudden surprises, we will be aware of monthly expenses, how much cash is needed and when, how much cash is available and when we can expect more cash in. This knowledge can help us arrange and manage bank overdrafts or short-term loan structures.

We should have audit procedures that prevent excess stockholdings, procedures to sell excess stock and raise revenues, security and fraud arrangements to prevent leakage.

We can increase sales through sales promotions, sell off existing stock, and buy in stock to take advantage of added activity.

Trust everyone but check everything to ensure cash is going where it should. Eliminate all risks and opportunity for theft.

Make cuts where we can afford too but don't push up costs and lose efficiency. Keep knowledge workers.

Cut all overtime and communicate with employees.

Reconsider any capital expenditure. Sell unwanted fixtures, fittings, machinery and vehicles etc.

Call in all outstanding monies. Don't give credit unless it's an approved loan. Be careful with suppliers as bad news spreads like wildfire, we don't want to lose our credit arrangements or our suppliers trust.

Restructuring existing debt can be an option. Also, trust mechanisms can be an effective method of cheap loans and reducing tax liabilities.

Cash leverage

How may existing cash reserves be used to grow opportunity?

Leverage is an investment technique in which you use a small amount of your own money to make an investment of much larger value. In that way, leverage gives you significant financial power.

For example, if you borrow 90% of the cost of a home, you are using the leverage to buy a much more expensive property than you could have afforded by paying cash.

If you sell the property for more than you borrowed, the profit is entirely yours. The reverse is also true. If you sell at a loss, the amount you borrowed is still due and the entire loss is yours.

Buying stock on margin is a type of leverage, as is buying a futures or options contract.

Leveraging can be risky if the underlying instrument doesn't perform as you anticipate. At the very least, you may lose your investment principal plus any money you borrowed to make the purchase.

With some leveraged investments, you could be responsible for even larger losses if the value of the underlying product drops significantly.

Sales Process - Protect

Sales order (internal)
Sales invoice for customer (internal)
Purchase order (internal)

Confirmation of order (external supplier)
Delivery advice note (external supplier)
Delivery note (external supplier)

Goods Received Note (internal)
Dispatch note (internal) ensure customer has paid for the goods prior to raising dispatch note.
Customer Delivery Note (internal)

Security

What strategies need to be in place to protect hard earned rewards from diminishing?

Investment

Can we invest in stocks?

Tax

Pay as little as possible, there's no moral obligation to pay tax, this will kill a business, less tax means more to invest and grow.

Reliefs / Allowances

Ensure all legal reliefs and allowances are applied to revenues by using skilled accountants.

Liabilities

Pay liabilities in a manner that protects cash flow and maintains fluid supplier networks

Schemes

Careful with schemes, anything called a scheme probably doesn't work or will end up costing you more.

Insurance

Offset the risk of uncertainty

Interest free loans

Money that is available at very favourable rates, partners, trust funds etc

Stock

This is future cash, prevent stock damage and pilferage, and keep stocks to a minimum to retain cashflow in the business

Losses

Should be offset and protected against

Compensation

Not possible to offset compensation orders against business losses. Raise possible risks through research and meetings.

Legal costs

Can spiral out of control, aim for business efficacy rather than legal argument.

Utilities

Source the best prices for gas, electricity, telephone and water etc

Fraud

Protect against organised criminal activity to defraud your business

Audit systems

Regular checks to monitor issues

Networks

Business is all about people, customers, suppliers, partners, stakeholders and these networks must be protected.

Intangible assets

Goodwill is the most valuable business asset and often unaccounted for. This is because we can't see intangible assets.

Time

Time Management, leverage and waste.

Often when we examine what we think we do against what we actually do we are surprised at the reality. One of the best examples of what we think we do compared to what we actually do is how we spend our time.

There are simple ways to examine time and we can start by making a time log to determine exactly how we spend our time. This way we can see exactly where time can be saved and where more effective use of time can be made. Then by improving how we spend our time we can efficiency and effectiveness that provide economic benefits for the company and employees. For example, improved working conditions, improved profits and more work / life balance.

- Time Management, Leverage & Waste
- Business Life Cycle
- Succession Planning,
- Exit Strategy
- Work / Life Balance
- Health & Vitality

Time management

- How can we do the things we do more efficiently

Time Leverage

- How can we get 10 hours work from 8 hours

Time Waste

- Where in our processes can we prevent time wasting

Stress (And Entrepreneur Capital)

Stress is caused when we don't have enough time to achieve results to the standard that we have set ourselves. In business this often means our plans have faltered, we failed to measure important tangible assets and intangible assets and were unable to take corrective action as necessary. One possible reason is our focus. Often, we focus on the cash-flow through the business and try to ensure liabilities are met. However, when we focus on just one type of capital, we are only managing a small part of the business and as goals are missed this affects the stress levels of entrepreneurs and the entrepreneur team. Having investment capital and a great idea for a business is just the start, with money and an idea alone all we have is a venture possibility, to grow a business we need 5 sorts of capital.

Entrepreneur Capital is someone or, a team of people, who are able to bring together all of the 'resources necessary' to solve the problem and develop a solution. Without entrepreneur capital, the ability to recognize opportunity and master the types of Business capital the venture will never 'get off the ground'.

Human Capital is the ideas in people's heads that make the idea and the solution and identify how all this can happen and deliver solutions for customers. Without a constant flow of ideas, the competition will leave us behind, we have to continuously change to meet the changing business landscapes, or we will lose market share that is very difficult to re-gain.

Structural capital is how we motivate people to move from a place of dissatisfaction to a more pleasurable place. This is achieved through systems, policies, procedures and other ways to replicate actions that create income streams and provide leverage and scale. This is how we grow. Without structure the business will not grow and will eventually die as liabilities outstrip cash-flow.

Network Capital is all the business relationships we make through the venture. There are many types of relationships, with customers, employees, suppliers and other stakeholders. Some of the relationships are very loose such as the passing customer we never see again while other relations are heavily contracted to protect the business survival. Without relationships the business will die, no-one to sell to, no-one to buy from, poor reputation and no credibility.

Financial Capital is an all-encompassing category for many types of business finance. Financial capital includes initial funding which may be personal capital investment, grants, loans or other credit terms. Once in the business cash is used to buy the means of production, research and development, advice, property, tools and machinery, raw materials, and to pay liabilities such as utility companies, employees, creditors, interest on loans, fuel and taxes and yourself. However, if we only focus on what we have to pay we will run out of cash quickly and running out of cash is the reason businesses fail. Key strategies include early identification of income streams. This means we can develop a financial plan to ensure spending is relative to cash-flow. Cash flow is a top concern and plans must focus on expected sales revenue with a sales forecast to ensure the revenue from sales of products and services meets expectations. Plans must be monitored frequently, every hour if necessary to ensure levels of cash-flow and margins are on track and any deviations must be corrected.

We often view financial capital, as the meaning for a business and it's easy to understand why as money is tangible and easy to count, track and measure. Whereas other types of capital (Entrepreneur, Human, Structural and Network capital) are intangible and much more difficult for the inexperienced to measure and account for. But easy when we know how, both to measure and improve the venture activities but also to understand how intangibles contribute to our financial success.

These types of issues require careful planning whether the business is a start-up or a mature organisation as running out of cash means sure death. But also, mismanagement of other types of capital means the business will not grow and

Stressors for entrepreneurs include:

1. Cash-flow
2. Personal financial reward
3. Too few contacts who can relate to entrepreneur experience
4. Difficult partners or investors
5. Competition
6. Confidence and loneliness

It's difficult to advise how to stay ahead of soul destroying stress levels but here are three questions we can ask ourselves that can help new entrepreneurs and start-up's to correct deviances against plan.

1. How available is start-up capital?
None/Scarce/Difficult to attain/ Easily accessible

2. How would you change your business funding if you started today?
Use the same strategy / More outside investors / Less outside investors

3. How would you describe your growth expectations?
Ahead of forecast / On track / Behind on forecast

The secret to control stress is to develop plans and set goals with realistic standards and deadlines. The greater the possibility of achieving something to the required standard within set timescales means the likelihood that stress will be controlled.

Exit Strategies

When building the business think about letting go at some stage and along the entrepreneur journey focus on the people who will take over from you, give them responsibilities early to ensure transitions are smooth when they are necessary. This will enable you to focus on the big picture, enjoy the ride, and be involved for longer and able to move easily into a more relaxed lifestyle. In effect you will have let go of the business in all but a tacit presence. This makes it easier for a buyer to take over and run your business without you in it and that is exactly what potential investors are looking for.

- Management Buy out
- Mergers & Acquisition
- Sell (whole or part)
- Failure / Bankruptcy

Prepare for Retirement Income

The secret is to find cash generating streams that will fund your retirement and one way of doing this is to invest in property and let these to tenants. You will always have the capital investment to realise should you wish and will also have a rental income monthly.

Networking

There are many networking events around cities as new and old businesses search for the next contact that will help benefit their business, these type of contacts are highly valuable as the relationships are reciprocal and we all rely on each other's survival to some extent, this helps achieve longevity for all concerned. Particularly, a benefit to a seasoned entrepreneur as often new and old businesses can benefit from your experience as a mentor or adviser providing a consultancy income.

Write Books

We each have a story to tell, how we got where we did, industry secrets, experiences with people that shaped our live and an audience of new entrepreneurs hungry for knowledge. Writing books is a great way to pass on experience and help self-mentor a new generation of entrepreneurs. This can lead to online courses, webinar and eBooks that provide alternative incomes.

Streamline the Business

Businesses that are automated, fully independent from their owners and rely on systems and processes provide more certainty for investors as they are less risky and attract higher financial valuations. Aim to document procedures and automate where possible, this provides leverage and certainty.

Employ and Develop a Great Team

Having a great team in place allows you to move effortlessly in and out of the business.

Pareto Principle or 80/20 Rule

80% of our income is derived from just 20% of our activity, therefore, we should try to identify exactly what we get paid for doing and do more of this.

Sell Parts of the Business

Some parts of your business may be more valuable to other companies than yours. Identifying unused warehouse space that can be let or sold may be a good example of reducing asset liability while creating an income.

Developing New Technologies

New technologies may give your business a boost, traditional businesses may develop new social media strategies or expand overseas using auction web site platforms.

Modify, Update or Repackage Products

Changing business landscapes often dictate trends in consumer buying behaviour. Re-launching old products in new and exciting ways can lift tired products and increase margins.

Franchise

Consider franchising your business as this allows new people to embark on an entrepreneurial journey without the risk as there will be a tried and tested formula for success.

Grow the Business or Diversify

Finding new ways to grow your business is easier with a research and development team onboard, however, great ideas will also come from your employees when we know how to tap into this important resource.

Change / Turnaround

We can only change or turnaround a business when we know where we are and where we want to be. Research and analysis is a key ingredient.

Business life cycle.

It's your baby but it will outgrow you. 10 years if we are lucky to survive year 1, then up to year 5!

- We seek status quo however equilibrium is death
- Businesses have a life cycle (10 years example)
- Products and services also come and go with fashions and other demands
- Competition does it faster, cheaper, lighter etc
- The only constant is change
- We must reinvent our business just to survive

Succession Planning:

- Who are the future leaders
- What happens should key workers leave today
- When do we expect leadership changes
- Plan for leadership change
- Promote from within where possible

Time & Business Failure

Hierarchy of Why Businesses Fail

NB: The percentage here represents what the businesses said were the reasons that contributed to business failure.

1. 50% Market need was not identified and tested - no need, no sales!
2. 30% Cash flow - running out of cash as a result of poor forecasting.
3. 20% Values alignment - vision & team, not the right team
4. 20% Competitive advantage - no edge! Beaten by competitors
5. 20% Profit margins - selling & cost price
6. 15% Inferior Products and services – value for money
7. 15% Poor Planning - No business model
8. 15% Marketing - exposure, costs & returns
9. 15% Relationships – Poor customer service
10. 15% Timing - grasping innovative opportunity, products mis-timed
11. 10% External focus - customers wants & needs
12. 10% Internal focus – relations
13. 10% Team, stakeholder - power/interest
14. 10% Changing Business Landscapes – Poor decisions or planning
15. 8% Values – lack of passion
16. 8% Location – Wrong location, no footfall, high costs, low sales
17. 8% Investors – no interest in providing financial support
18. 8% The Law – Becoming embroiled in legal challenges
19. 5% Networks – No or poor networks, no advisers or mentors
20. 5% Stress – stressed to the point of burn out
21. 5% Change – failing to throw away the plan

Reasons Businesses Fail or Survive		
Reason	**Failure**	**Survival Action**
Market Need	No need means no sales	Identify market / Gap analysis
Cashflow	Running out of cash	Cashflow forecasts, develop and review
Values Alignment	Vision & team, not the right team	Create a vision & ensure team has the same values
Competitive Advantage	Beaten by competitors	Business case, Create a USP, Benefit Statement
Profit Margins	Sold to cheaply	Develop a pricing strategy
Inferior Products	Poor value for money	Price must reflect value
Planning	No plans or poorly researched	Plan everything
Marketing	No exposure, high costs / low returns	Develop productive marketing strategy
Relationships	No networks, poor customer relations	Build and Maintain Reputation
Timing	Products mis-timed	Grasp Opportunity, don't Procrastinate
External Focus	Must identify customer's wants & needs	Sell to customer's needs and create wants
Internal Focus	Employee relations	Agree terms & conditions, monitor
Team / Stakeholders	Low power / low interest	Create highly motivated high performing teams
Changing Business Environment	Failing to change or poor decision-making	Predict and react to change requirements
Values	Lack of passion	Change the vision or the team
Location	Wrong location, low footfall, high costs	Location, Location, Location
Investors	No interest in providing financial support	Review vision & competencies
Law	Embroiled in legal fights	Focus on business efficacy not law
Networks	Poor networks, no advisors or mentors	Develop networks and find a mentor
Stress	Stressed to the point of burnout	Plan, set objectives, monitor, review, action
Change	Failure to throw away the plan	Know when to quit

The benefit of this table is apparent. Mentors must focus on the top end of the table and arguably, this will mean huge strides can be made to reduce business failures.

For example:

1. Ensure new ventures identify and test the market need.
2. Financial planning must be robustly executed.
3. The business values and all stakeholders must be aligned.
4. There must be inimitable competitive advantage, don't compete on price.
5. Ensure selling price accounts for all costs and provides value for money.

New entrepreneurs must use Mentors as an asset for knowledge, experience and networks.

Work Life Balance

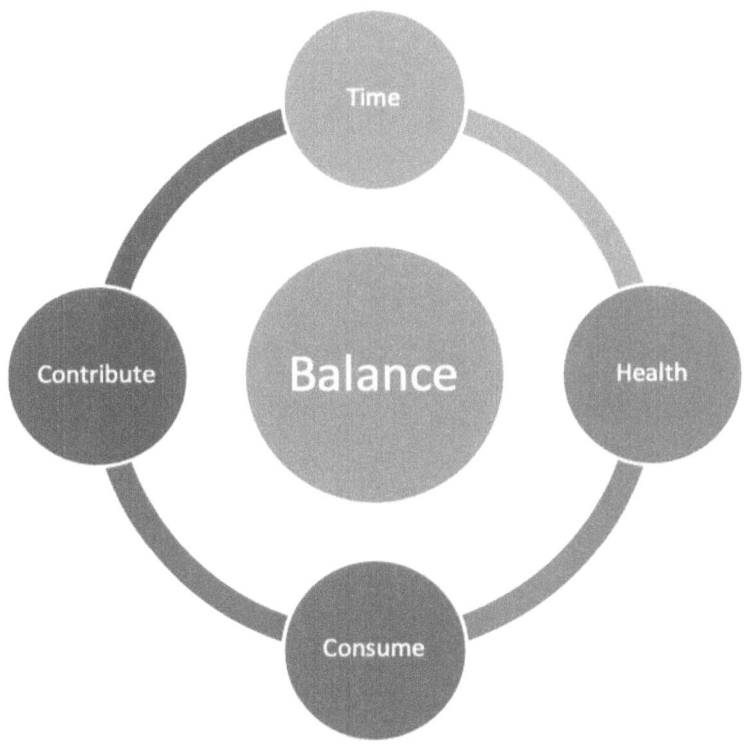

Work / Life Balance is Subjective:

- What are we prepared to 'give and take' to achieve our 'wants and needs' in work / life balance?
- More of one lifestyle choice has a negative effect on other areas.

Time: Work / Life Balance	
Contribution / Give **Family, Friends, Social, Gifts, Advice, Charity, Smiles, Hugs, Time**	**Time / Wants** More Time, Save time Distort time, Make time SMART decisions Time for ME!
Consume / Take **Possessions, Clothes, Jewelry, Cars, Houses, Cash, Food, Drink.** **Work, hobbies & vacations**	**Health / Needs** Quality of life, Longevity. Great diet, Pain & Stress free, Exercise, Spiritual, Reduced risk of heart & liver disease, stroke, cancer, diabetes.

The Protect Model

PROTECT	
Process	Recipes for success, products, patents etc
Risk Reporting Relations	Build reputation and credibility by identifying and removing risks and a reproting strategy of full transparency
Operations	Property, premises, machinery and tools etc
Tactics	Tactical objectives and the means of achievement = competitive advantage
Employees	Contracts, remuneration, health & safety etc
Capital	Cash generation, leverage, investment, tax etc
Time	Management, leverage and waste

The Ingredients of the Financial Driver

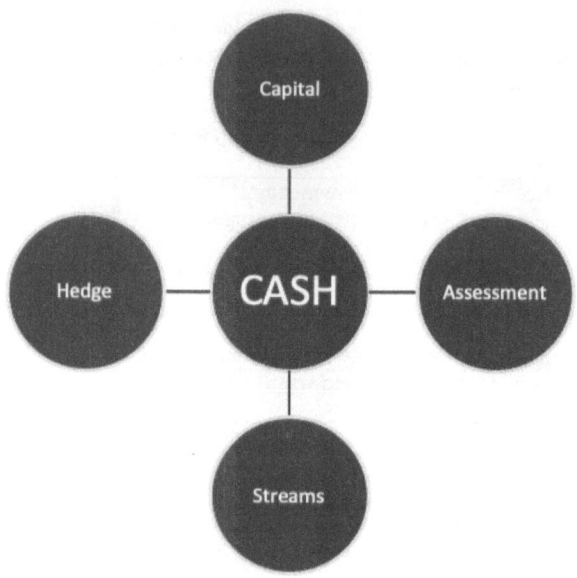

Financial Resources (CASH)

Required for businesses to start, exist, survive and deliver solutions and provide social benefits.

Entrepreneur Catch 22

Entrepreneurs want and need tangibles
And tangibles are a result of intangibles
And intangibles are created from tangibles

Financial Capital Role & Tasks

CASH	
Capital	Money or other assets owned, available or sales forecast that can be used to meet liabilities or for investing
Assessment	Aim to identify and assess the risks regarding ability satisfy liabilities as they fall due. Assess financial plans and contingencies and the ability to eliminate and reduce risks. Quantify the financial resources found necessary to mitigate risks. Plan the ability of strategies to provide adequate and regular cash-flow.
Streams	Identify and develop continuous, variable and regular sources of financial income.
Hedge	Safeguard the business and the venture rewards against financial loss and create a buffer to reduce risks in case of unforeseen opportunities or adverse circumstances.

The CASH Mnemonic

Capital
Assessment
Streams
Hedge

Capital

Money or other assets owned, available or sales forecast that can be used to meet liabilities or for investing

Assessment

Aim to identify and assess the risks regarding ability satisfy liabilities as they fall due.

Assess financial plans and contingencies and the ability to eliminate and reduce risks.

Quantify the financial resources found necessary to mitigate risks.

Plan the ability of strategies to provide adequate and regular cash-flow.

Streams

Identify and develop continuous, variable and regular sources of financial income.

Hedge

Safeguard the business and the venture rewards against financial loss and create a buffer to reduce risks in case of unforeseen opportunities or adverse circumstances.

Entrepreneur Action Model

The Entrepreneur Action Model demonstrates the entrepreneur environment. We have 2 axis, the vertical axis, Stability or static efficiency where the organisation strives for perfection, as where everything is in order and working to its optimum the organisation will be an efficient, effective and economic producer. However, if the organisation remains in stability it will die.

In reality, all economies move to the right and towards entrepreneur action, new products and processes. This is driven by the wants and needs of external factors such as customers, suppliers and competitors and internal factors such as R&D, employees, management and staff leavers. This creates tension in the organisation and demand for new products or services or new ways of doing things and as a result, change.

Entrepreneurs are constantly immersed in this environment, as inventors they discover constraints and solutions, as leaders they achieve results and as managers, they protect venture rewards.

Entrepreneurs have entrepreneur spirit and as such they seek out change, they ask what is wrong with the current situation and how can we do it better. The entrepreneur environment is in a constant state of flux as demonstrated below:

Entrepreneur Action Model notes:

➢ Comfort zone represents the economic theory of Static Efficiency.

➢ Entrepreneur action in economics is Dynamic Efficiency.

➢ The 4 Entrepreneur roles of Coordinator, Inventor, Leader and Manager:

➢ Organise represents coordinator action
➢ Discover represents innovation
➢ Achieve represents leadership and motivation
➢ Protect represents value management

➢ Internal rivalry represents employee tensions
➢ External rivalry represents demand for change from suppliers and customers

➢ Change represents the economic theory of Creative Destruction

Paul Clargo's Entrepreneur Action Model

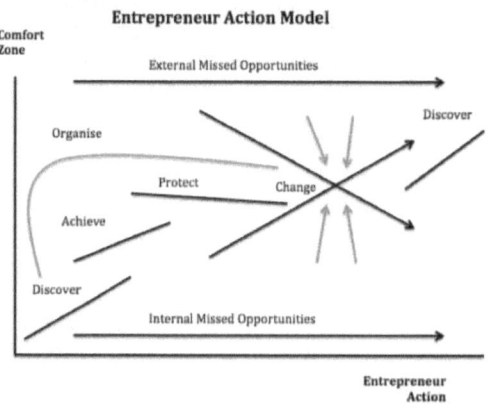

- Stability in economics is static efficiency or equilibrium, remaining here is death.
- Entrepreneur action in economics is dynamic efficiency and continuous progress.
- The 4 Entrepreneur roles of Coordinator, Inventor, Leader and Manager
- These roles drive entrepreneurs to organise, discover, achieve and protect.
- Internal & External rivalry from employees, competitors and customers.
- Change, where chaos converges in economics this is Creative Destruction.

The Problem with Entrepreneur Research

The problem with entrepreneur research is that there's not enough research and what exists is unreliable. It's unreliable for a number of reasons, primarily, because of its complexity and also the narrow approach of existing research that mostly focuses on the successful entrepreneur with the aim to learn how to do what they do. This narrow approach explains why there is not enough entrepreneur research, that is, by focus on the entrepreneur instead of a multi-disciplinary approach means there are huge gaps in the research because studies do not take into account all human behaviours that lead to entrepreneur action. This means many aspects of human behaviour, in relation to entrepreneurship, are left undiscovered. As a result of these knowledge gaps, government activity that supports and is aimed at driving entrepreneur organisations to produce economic activity, new products, jobs and other social benefits is underperforming.

Another problem with entrepreneur research is bias. This bias is because of the special person argument, where entrepreneurs are viewed as portraying certain special traits that sets them apart from non-entrepreneurs. This theory is difficult to prove, entrepreneurs are everywhere, every race, every religion, every country, every industry and while the trait theory suggests entrepreneurs are just born this way, many entrepreneurs drive success through developing and training employees to behave in a way that aligns employees with corporate culture based on attitudes and skills. Thus, by conjecture, they argue we can train employees to be entrepreneurial within entrepreneur organisations but there is a pseudo-denial of being able to train people to be entrepreneurs (in some countries). There is a denial of failure or responsibility for failure but an overwhelming willingness amongst entrepreneurs to take credit for success and then failures are often revisited as important learning experiences that led to success. But there's no success in failure and failure is no success at all. Failure is a cost. Maybe this is the correct approach. But an entrepreneur who wants to leverage economic activity may disagree with this doubtful and rhetorical assumption. So, the problem to start with is overcoming the self-serving bias of entrepreneurs and those who study entrepreneurs and suggest unreliably unproven theories about entrepreneurs and entrepreneurship because of the inherent bias. It's not anyone's fault, no-one is to blame, entrepreneurship is too complex to be left to biased admirers and the successful who probably didn't record how they got there anyway. But mankind needs to understand how entrepreneurial people identify value, create value, deliver value and protect value. How do they spot an opportunity, solve the problem, develop a product or service and exploit this for gain and reward? Some people have bags of personality but without an idea they won't be entrepreneurial, ideas alone require implementation to return a reward and to leverage the results there must be a process that can be replicated around the world, and this requires relationships with employees, suppliers, marketing companies, investors etc. Therefore, this requires a holistic approach as to focus only on personality and cash does not result in entrepreneur action.

Can we learn this entrepreneur skill and pass it on to others? Entrepreneurs believe they can in the form of mentoring, so why can't universities or schools or parents, what's the secrets? I think amongst the entrepreneur research there is reliable and unreliable evidence. I also think that there is vital evidence that remains undiscovered. I would encourage researchers to throw out unreliable evidence and to broaden the quest for answers beyond the successful entrepreneur and encourage researchers to look elsewhere for evidence of entrepreneur action and its meaning. This book will aim to seek-out and provide some of the answers to help support entrepreneurship such as **is it a lack of funding or ideas or a lack of entrepreneur spirit, or a shortage of entrepreneurs.**

My Assumptions

My assumptions are that there is a link between entrepreneurs who pull everything together, who are innovative, achievers and managers of value. There seems to be a link between entrepreneurship and 'intellectual capital accounting (IC) that is the subject of measuring ideas, processes and relationships. This link is not discussed anywhere in the literature of entrepreneurship nor IC and this I find very surprising. Arguably, the more exposure an entrepreneur has to the skills of their craft then the higher the probability of opportunity recognition, the entrepreneur leap and the likelihood of venture survival and success! I believe that entrepreneurship should be a way of life. In fact, I believe everyone is a born entrepreneur, some people choose the entrepreneurial path early, others as grey entrepreneurs, some are better than others and many choose not to pursue entrepreneurship! Others are entrepreneurial then go to school and are taught to get jobs! I assume, everyone has entrepreneurial capability to some degree, be it organizing, leading, managing, creating or protecting resources etc. This does not mean everyone is an entrepreneur, however, it does support the assumption that many people are probably capable of supporting entrepreneurial activity and that exposure to entrepreneurship may provide a referent for latent entrepreneurs to make the entrepreneur leap at some time. It also means that we can learn to think in an entrepreneurial way much the same as other professionals learn their craft. Design thinking for entrepreneurs!

For example:

- Law students learn to think about workable legal strategies.
- Tax consultants learn to think about tax evasion and tax avoidance.
- Accountancy students learn to think about improving financial performance.
- Project managers learn to think about delivering project objectives.
- Medical students learn to think about disease, remedies and surgical procedures.
- Civil engineers learn to think about building bridges and roads.
- Builders learn how to think about creating homes.
- Entrepreneurs learn to think about finding and exploiting opportunities.

Born or Made

Are entrepreneurs born or made? This is an age-old argument and there is no right or wrong answer as long as there are entrepreneur's then that is a great result. However, if we are to have more entrepreneurs we have to understand as much as we can about them as, understanding entrepreneurs will help us design entrepreneur thinking programmes.

Lord Alan Sugar:

"It doesn't matter which business school you go to or what books you read, you can't go into Boots and buy a bottle of entrepreneurial juice - entrepreneurial spirit is something you are born with."

Great words, but the research does not support this view, arguably, everyone has some entrepreneur spirit, and some people have more entrepreneur spirit, more knowledge, more experience, more ideas and more investment opportunity. Arguably, this is because they think differently, they are not satisfied with the norm and are willing to challenge the status quo and provide solutions. Having arrived at the consensus of opinion that entrepreneurs think differently this is a great result. We can develop training programmes that help people think differently and leverage knowledge through focus on improving our knowledge and its application. The question is are we able to 'bottle it' (sell it in Boots) and share it with others and then influence entrepreneur thinking to a large enough degree to drive entrepreneur activity and create more jobs. What else must be discovered to make an entrepreneur environment and drive the probability of venture success?

Research has shown that economists and lawyers and those well-educated have the highest propensity to be entrepreneurial! They are hardly born entrepreneurial lawyers or economists but their training builds confidence and high earnings. But what about doctors who start practices, scientists that develop drugs and pharmaceutical companies, racing drivers who develop green technology for town cars, swimmers and footballers that develop fashion ranges, bricklayers who become house-builders and sellers of homes and, entrepreneurs are they any different, somewhere along the way there is a brain fest, information being elicited and interpreted according to the mood of the receiver and the environment and maybe put to use at some future point in time. It's non-sensical to think of anyone being born into anything,

While people will start businesses as and when the circumstances are right for them, training and exposure to entrepreneurship will provide the toolbox ready to be accessed and applied to the relevant situation, much like a carpenter will choose a chisel or a saw or a hammer depending on the stage of work to be focused on. Entrepreneurs adapt their skills to take advantage and make the best of an opportunity.

Entrepreneurs & Economic Drivers

The 'entrepreneur leap' is the point where an entrepreneur decides to start a venture and run with an idea. To me this is 'convergent thinking', a point in time where attitude, knowledge and skills meet, opportunity, environment and resources. The entrepreneur believes they can pull all this together to exploit the solution and make a profit. From my research it is apparent that the driver is either the solution to a problem or the money that can be made from the exploitation of the solution. The belief is so strong the entrepreneur then makes the 'entrepreneurial leap'.

Entrepreneurs & Economic Drivers

Entrepreneurs & Economic Drivers	
Attitude	Opportunity
Knowledge	Resources
Skills	Environment

Arguably, the entrepreneur leap is a coming together of attitude, knowledge, skills, opportunity, resources and environment. But understanding the drivers of entrepreneurship is very difficult because of the many variables amongst people, industries and circumstances that drive or prevent the decision to make the 'entrepreneurial leap'. However, breaking down the ingredients of entrepreneurship helps us to understand the thinking process and to develop processes to leverage resources and scale the solution. Just like any product solution. However, there are also very strong environmental factors.

One of the biggest environmental factors is the availability of jobs. In the UK during the recession from 2007 to 2012 there was an unprecedented increase in self-employment due to the job shortage and maybe the availability of redundancy money to fund start-ups as people with no income and no job prospects have little choice but to make the entrepreneurial leap. However, an Australian study found that capital is not a barrier to entrepreneurship it is the shortage of ideas that poses the problem for growing entrepreneurs. The evidence suggests that money ideas and environmental circumstances are all factors in entrepreneurship. But are these new entrepreneurs already potential entrepreneurs or did they suddenly realise they weren't employees after all, and they were born entrepreneurs? Arguably, circumstances made them act, they needed an income and decided to take charge of income generation through launching entrepreneurial ventures and then coming up with an idea. I have found that entrepreneurs start businesses for two reasons, because they want to and because they need to. Starting a business to satisfy a 'want' may relate to the great idea whereas 'need' is more likely to be a desperate attempt to fund physiological needs and each reason provides a different motivation factor.

When considering economic conditions, we may expect more entrepreneurs during economic upturns when times are good but recent studies in 2015 have found that as jobs are more plentiful entrepreneurial ventures become less attractive leading to fewer start-ups. This may be due to the risk of entrepreneur investment compared with the security of a tried and tested employer. Or the difficulty of running an entrepreneur venture, finding support, training and investment and dealing with business regulations maybe for the first time, may be too great and too complex at the point of start-up. All these barriers may lead to a reduction in new start-up ventures but also the biggest barrier may be the high risk to investment considering that there is a high first year failure rate and short-term difficulties up to year 5. It's not until after year 5 that business survival rates increase substantially, and entrepreneurs survive and succeed in often the toughest of environments and this is often the only study focus.

Therefore, entrepreneurs are not always entrepreneurs at some stage they were at college, university, in good jobs or poorly paid employment or unemployed or building a successful entrepreneur venture. But it seems people display entrepreneur thinking and entrepreneur potential before being successful entrepreneurs. Thus, people are always potential entrepreneurs. But we don't know where the next idea or the next entrepreneur will come from or when they will emerge. People with an identified 'need' in the form of income, financial capital to invest and an idea they 'want' to share, are all referents that make entrepreneurial leaps more probable and may explain why there was an increase in the self-employed during the recession.

Equilibrium v Chaos	
Equilibrium	**Chaos**
Comfort Zone	Dissatisfaction
Status Quo	Change
Static Efficiency	**Dynamic Efficiency**
Order	Opportunity
Safe	New Wants and Needs
Satisfying existing markets	Risk
Perceived pleasure	Perceived Pain

However, there are some people who decide they want to be entrepreneurs as a career. Is it about control, are we happy to let others control us and then suddenly decide we can't work for others anymore and have to take-back control? This also demonstrates people may prefer employment but when the need arises and tensions converge why do people exercise their inherent entrepreneurial tendencies and what makes entrepreneurs at some point, revert to employment?

The evidence suggests that our entrepreneurial propensity grows and recedes depending upon our economic 'wants' and 'needs' and environmental factors. In countries where there is no state support 'you work, or you don't eat' and this is a huge motivator to escape poverty through entrepreneur thinking.

Although much time and effort is spent arguing over whether entrepreneurs are born or made, we do know that these same entrepreneurial tendencies have similarities all around the globe, no matter where we live, being self-employed and running small businesses is not always about making millions, it's often about basic human physiological needs, survival or just wanting to help others.

In my research, I found an economics theory of entrepreneurship that stated 'all people have the right to be entrepreneurial and to receive the rewards for their entrepreneurial efforts'. Thus, the fact all people are entitled to be entrepreneurs suggest that people are naturally entrepreneurial. Entrepreneurship is a natural characteristic of humans and up until 1985 entrepreneurs had never been considered to be a special type of person.

This is supported by the fact entrepreneurs seem to come from every possible background, this demonstrates there is something special about every person on this planet and an abundance of 'e-juice'. It's more likely that referents that align a person's skills and values are a catalyst for entrepreneurship rather than a person having been born with a higher order entrepreneurial spoon in their mouth!

Thus, we may have an opportunity to influence people's entrepreneurial skills and values and consider how environmental referents may be exploited as entrepreneurial opportunity. In essence, the research suggests we can think like entrepreneurs when we understand them and if we understand them, we can drive entrepreneurship, improve the possibility of opportunity recognition, encourage the entrepreneur leap, increase the probability of venture survival and increase economic activity, jobs and social benefits. There are great humanitarian benefits for supporting entrepreneurship and discovering how entrepreneurs think and documenting this entrepreneur thinking process.

Shaping, Making, Driving

5 Questions

Are entrepreneurs born with cash or do they make cash?
Are entrepreneurs born coordinators or do they learn to identify value?

Are entrepreneurs born inventors or do they learn to create value?

Are entrepreneurs born leaders or do they learn to deliver value?
Are entrepreneurs born managers or do they learn to protect value?

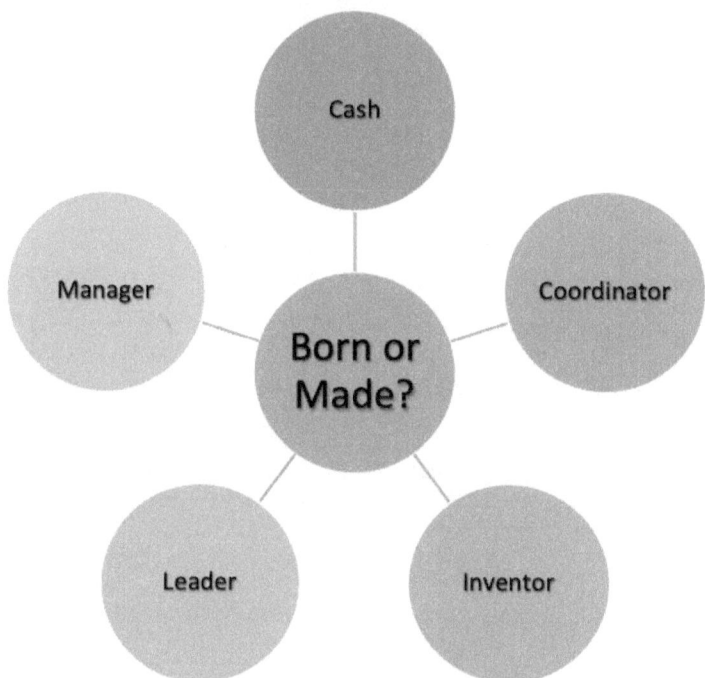

Who are entrepreneurs?

When we think of who is an entrepreneur images may come to mind of successful people like Richard Branson, Steve Jobs or Warren Buffet. The one thing these people have in common is that they are all different. So, who is an entrepreneur? A lot of studies into entrepreneurship examine successful entrepreneurs and while this glorifies individual success and researchers who admire entrepreneurs this does not really help the development of entrepreneurship as a subject. This is because of bias, denial and an absence of reliable evidence of how these successful entrepreneurs in the study became successful.

Trying to cut through the spin of publicity is very difficult as successful entrepreneurs promote themselves in a positive manner to drive their businesses and build positive public relations. Therefore, arguably, a study about a successful entrepreneur may be interesting but from a development point of view this is unhelpful and promotes limiting beliefs and in fact entrepreneurs deplore limiting beliefs as this fetters achievement and growth. However, we can't move away from the fact that many entrepreneur studies mention the born or made debate, personality traits or behavioural characteristics, all of which apply to the entrepreneur in some way being a special type of person with entrepreneurial prowess.

Many traits are found in entrepreneurs and ordinary people and the position of traits is heavily criticised from both angles. However, traits are important, some traits have been proven to make a difference to entrepreneurship while some traits are not as important. Either way, traits and personality alone is not enough to be a successful entrepreneur and other entrepreneur ingredients may also be necessary. But entrepreneur traits are interesting, and personality is a good focal point.

The question, 'are entrepreneurs born or made' may have been misconstrued as well. Does it mean they are born with entrepreneur characteristics; they are full of ideas, or does it mean they are born with the financial resource that makes entrepreneurship possible at some point later in life, (perhaps after training to take over the family business). Equally, does it mean an entrepreneurial mindset has been made or financial resources have been made? So many different interpretations by many people and therefore the born or made question is difficult if not impossible to solve. However, maybe it's what entrepreneurs do rather than who they are that makes them think in an entrepreneurial way.

The 'Special Person' Entrepreneur.

Throughout my research I have found entrepreneurs to be normal people able to face uncertainty and risk, make unique assumptions of responsibility and to justify profits, in essence entrepreneurs are coordinators, inventors, leaders and managers, who organise, discover, achieve and protect. And as I found, not until modern times around 1985 do we see the emergence of the entrepreneur as a special person.

The scientific evidence does not support a special person theory and economists and this research prefer to predict entrepreneurs to be people in general who have the ability to identify value from constraints and solve the problem for profit, to organise and create value through innovation, to motivate and coordinate resources to move from a position of dissatisfaction to a new more favourable position and deliver value and to secure gains and protect value.

Entrepreneurs act as coordinators to organise and unify inventors, leaders and managers who create the vision, motivate employees and leverage resources, and secure financial and non-financial rewards.

Therefore, entrepreneurs and entrepreneurial teams are always all of the following 4 roles. They are coordinators of inventors, leaders and managers and these roles are found in every organisation and every area of business and social life, and we see these characteristics everyday amongst children, young people and their activities once we know what to look for.

In everything that people do daily we act out the roles that make the 'special entrepreneur person', we have ideas, organise resources, move from 'A' to 'B' and share and reward ourselves, it's human nature, take a look around. The difference may only be the application of investment and risk.

Entrepreneurs take a risk when they act as coordinators and provide the enthusiasm, motivation and knowledge that facilitates entrepreneurship through their ability to identify opportunities from the chaotic distribution of resources in the market.

They act as inventors and must possess the means of being innovative enough to provide creativity and imagination in solutions.

They must motivate for change and lead to stay ahead of competitors by anticipating market changes and fluctuations that mean a shift in consumer demands.

Finally, they must act as managers and collect, store and make re-usable knowledge about market data and venture gains in a way that generates and maintains profits despite having to reach profit making decisions about the coordination of scarce resources.

When we look at something in a different way we will achieve different results, examining successful entrepreneurs glorifies entrepreneurs as 'special entrepreneur people' because of what they have achieved, we want to figure out the processes that led to the success of the entrepreneur rather than genetic DNA of each entrepreneur.

We are trying to find the normal things that people do each day that can lead to entrepreneur activity, things like chaotic environments that we must organise, sometimes in new and exciting ways, the motivation and drive we need to carry out that task and the satisfaction we feel from life's rewards. By breaking down entrepreneur success to natural human behaviours we are beginning to make some sense of the complexity of the sophisticated entrepreneur.

So, what makes and shapes entrepreneurs, its life events, experiences, influences, choices, interpretations, our mentors, education and environmental drivers and barriers or referents and much more.

Entrepreneur is a Normal Person (with Special thinking!)

Therefore, we begin to see a picture of entrepreneurs who identify constraints and then coordinate the bringing together of resources in an organised manner to innovate solutions, achieve goals and manage rewards. As a whole this may be a normal person who exercises entrepreneur mastery.

When we start thinking of the entrepreneur as a normal person we can start to move forward and progress the subject. Thinking of the special person entrepreneur as in the 'Exceptional Personality Theory' makes it difficult to make any scientific sense of entrepreneurs. The world does not stop to wait for an entrepreneur, problems issues and constraints appear constantly and there are always people around ready and willing to provide solutions.

However, some people are undoubtedly better than other people at spotting opportunities and providing solutions, and this is what we need to bottle. What are the ingredients for opportunity recognition, innovation, achievement and rewards? When we can identify the ingredients, we are able to improve them. The reality is that entrepreneurs are everywhere, discovering ways to drive economic activity through products and services that meet the wants and needs of consumers.

Entrepreneurs are improving our lives by improving their own entrepreneur attitude, knowledge and skills. **Entrepreneurship is too important to be left to chance, the chance that someone will come up with an idea and leap into entrepreneurship.**

Entrepreneurs are Normal People

I have found all the following authors ignore limiting beliefs and consider the entrepreneur is a normal person:

Adam Smith, Cantillon, Schumpeter, Jean-Battiste Say, Knight, Casson, Kirzner, Marshall, Denison, Weber, Martinelli, Sombart, Nietzsche, Santarelli, Pesciarelli, Marx, David Ricardo, Engels, Metcalfe, Scranton and I include myself in this list as a believer of the entrepreneur as an ordinary person.

Thus, when an entrepreneur is viewed as a normal person, we can find scientific answers that are repeatable. This means once we know the ingredients of entrepreneurship the growth of an entrepreneur can be influenced. The reason to exploit entrepreneurship in this way is that everyone has the right to be entrepreneurial and to receive the rewards from entrepreneurship.

Therefore, it's our duty to provide the opportunity to every person, schoolchild, student, employee and other adults to have the knowledge of entrepreneurial skills and ensure entrepreneurship is a choice. People should ignore the mystery and must believe an entrepreneur is a normal person with the attitude, knowledge and skills to execute entrepreneurial ideas in an extraordinary manner.

So, THINK BIG.

We need more businesses and more entrepreneurs so we must find ways to train normal people to be entrepreneurs there simply isn't enough jobs for those who need them. However, there must be a focus shift from trying to find them (the special person) to creating them.

Can entrepreneurship be taught?

Well, no one is born being able to do anything, we learn everything.

There are many different ways of learning and entrepreneurs tend to learn from experience, mainly because education systems are not yet on an entrepreneurial wavelength.

Therefore, there is an opportunity for a massive change in the way we promote entrepreneurship to our young people and create new futures and new jobs.

What Makes and Shapes Entrepreneurs?

So that we can change we need to know the ingredients of entrepreneurship, what makes and shapes entrepreneurs.

Shaping Entrepreneurs	
Attitude	Entrepreneur Nurturing & Nature
Knowledge	Schools, Colleges, University, Parents, Teachers, Media, Peers
Skills	Work, Events, Experiences
Resources	Entrepreneur Spirit, Mindset (Can Do Attitude)
Opportunity	Entrepreneur Leap
Environment	Entrepreneur Environment, Loose Structures
Support	Entrepreneur Diversity, Change & Group Think, Support, Mentors

Entrepreneur Culture

Nurturing and Nature & Developing an Entrepreneur Attitude

The USA produces more entrepreneurs than most other developed countries arguably because of attitudes to entrepreneurship that nurture young people in a way that trains them to think about self-employment and being whatever, they think they want to be. I saw USA early nurturing when some people inspired by Muhammad Ali took their children to his funeral to demonstrate that dreams can become reality no matter where you are from. In India, many poor children are fending for themselves on the streets and must be enterprising just to survive and they learn to survive in nature's hardest environment, often alone and afraid. The UK produces fewer than expected entrepreneurs, Wales, Scotland and Northern Ireland trail behind England although having similar types of entrepreneur programmes the attitudes toward personal ambition varies. In countries like Spain and Portugal there are fewer entrepreneurs and less emphasis on developing entrepreneurship. Therefore, it seems that entrepreneurship is dependent on not only nurture and nature but also environmental interruptions from both the economic environment and government enterprise support.

There are gaps in our entrepreneur knowledge and the disparity of entrepreneur culture around the world provides clues as to where our energy must be directed to have the best economic effect. Countries that leave entrepreneurship to nature out of poverty and hardship or nurture youngsters in belief produce the most entrepreneurs. Whereas countries that begin entrepreneurship at the mentoring stages produce fewer entrepreneurs. Therefore, it seems reasonably to conclude that developing entrepreneurs is a cultural issue rather than a special person issue. Development of entrepreneurs requires a cultural shift in approach to a nurturing type of education that provides opportunities at home and school for a positive approach to self-employment, entrepreneurship, intrapreneurship and employment. Career is a real choice and positive nurturing is a mature method of education.

The education and skills courses do not turn out entrepreneurs meaning it's highly likely that our schools, colleges and universities do not really relate to business in an entrepreneurial way. Business is not entrepreneurship, there are many self-employed businesspeople running businesses, but entrepreneurs are focused on scale. This is a big difference. Education should focus on developing the skills of an entrepreneur before teaching about running a business. However, education is not a barrier to entrepreneurship as there are many examples of successful businesspeople who have been disadvantaged in life because of a lack of education or an inability to learn in schools for a variety of reasons including for example undetected dyslexia. But we must learn from these variables and raise our game by thinking entrepreneurially to have an effect on the number of new businesses created.

However, education may be a barrier where investment is sought on a first entrepreneur venture. Banks and other creditors need to consider the risk of the lending and all positive experiences will help to convince people to lend or invest in you. For example, an entrepreneur with a track record of credibility approaching an investor may be considered on a different level to someone with an idea but no business experience. Of course, if you have the ability to invest in your own business then education is never an issue or a barrier to the entrepreneur leap but can be a barrier to venture success.

"Champions aren't made in gyms. Champions are made from something they have deep inside them, a desire, a dream and a vision. They have to have the skill and the will. But the will must be stronger than the skill.'

Muhammad Ali.

Therefore, champions have to have the skill to beat the equally skilled opposition but the greater 'WILL' makes the difference.

Education & MBA's

So, does an MBA provide the relevant business skills for entrepreneurship? Many students think so and often entrepreneurship is the reason for enrolling on an MBA. However, arguably the relevant business skills are not provided, MBA's focus in leadership, finance, marketing, strategy and operations, the content is academic but using business models and scenarios to expose issues and find solutions. Many MBA courses are filled with managers from large corporations, government departments such as tax or local government and relatively few private business candidates and even less people who have to take on the exorbitant fees themselves. Are these MBA courses turning out entrepreneurs or raising promotion prospects? There's no doubt that the content is stretching to the mind. MBA's teach us masterliness, a different way of thinking, analysing, application and, are life-changing experiences. The skills learned on an MBA are different to entrepreneurial skills but are a complementary life experience. MBA's obviously help some entrepreneurs start a venture but not others who may have their sights set on a career promotion.

I think an Entrepreneur Education provides, at best, business knowledge and specifically leadership and management prowess. This helps business leaders to analyse their business decisions from an academic perspective. However, arguably, entrepreneur perception is grown outside of the classroom and emerges specifically in situations that expose players to organising, innovating, leading and managing where the skill is complemented by the will to win and by conjecture, entrepreneurship is much wider than business, leadership and management courses taught in the 'gym.'

Entrepreneurship is a mix of many disciplines such as:

- Organising
- Innovation
- Leading
- Managing
- Business and Management
- Behavioural Sciences
- Criminology (Rule Breaking)
- Sociology
- Psychology
- Economics
- Taxation
- Psychiatry
- Accounting
- Knowledge Management
- Risk Management
- Change Management
- Intellectual Capital Accounting

However, as work experience builds credibility, owning assets demonstrates stability, an MBA or other similar standard of education is a badge of business understanding. With all three a potential entrepreneur may have a higher probability of obtaining much needed investment capital.

Who Would You Lend To?

Entrepreneur Lending Criteria	
Idea	Essential or Desirable or Irrelevant
Financial Assets	Essential or Desirable or Irrelevant
Non-financial Assets (Work processes)	Essential or Desirable or Irrelevant
Work Experience	Essential or Desirable or Irrelevant
Industry Knowledge Track Record	Essential or Desirable or Irrelevant
Reputation for Winning	Essential or Desirable or Irrelevant
Education / MBA	Essential or Desirable or Irrelevant
Business Experience	Essential or Desirable or Irrelevant
Entrepreneur Characteristics	Essential or Desirable or Irrelevant

MBA Tools

MBA's have the tools to assess businesses and the environment, business landscapes and assess competencies required to achieve the vision. An MBA proposing a business idea should have a good idea of the feasibility of the venture. However, unless there are other skills behind the venture such as work experience or cash then an MBA alone does not build complete credibility. MBA's do help some people, but their effect may be found more useful in larger companies, existing businesses, government or NGO's, rather than startups. Thus, some people believe MBA's do not fully address the needs of startup businesses and this may mean subject matter focuses on business skills rather than entrepreneurship. However, if you choose to be an entrepreneur it is probably better to be an educated one.

MBA's & Self-employment

MBA's aside, some research has shown high confidence and many entrepreneur ventures from academics and that dispels the theory that entrepreneurs are born, obviously at least some are made. So, there may be a correlation between academics and entrepreneurship. On a level playing field we would say that education does not hinder ambition, however, education may stifle entrepreneurs natural talent where they are focused on getting people into jobs rather than providing the skills to make a choice between employment and self-employment. I found university fails to turn out entrepreneurs in any great numbers and enquiries with one top ten university that runs entrepreneur courses advised me that the course resulted in no venture start-ups in 2014. Students say they enjoy rhetorical speeches from real entrepreneurs. Mentors. But why is it so difficult to grasp entrepreneurship in an education setting? Do we allow the economic future of our children to rest with unstructured teachings? Is this the only way? Scan around the university courses in entrepreneurship and MBA's and it becomes apparent that courses don't teach entrepreneurship at all. Many courses don't even include 'sales' programmes? Nor did I find courses that focus on the entrepreneur process or what entrepreneurs actually do. Coordinating, inventing, leading and managing or thinking like an entrepreneur!

Work Experience

Get a job with a positive entrepreneurially motivated company, where ideas are encouraged and valued. This will help understand sales, customer service, work structures, people's motivations and behaviours and the importance of work processes to leverage resources and scale the business to make a profit.

Entrepreneur Mindset.

Entrepreneur Mindset where is people seek out change to rectify discrepancies with the status quo, products that fall short of expectations, old systems that fail to deliver expected performance etc.

Events & Experiences Shape Entrepreneur Skills

Events and experiences that shape our lives can be interpreted in many ways that promote positivity and solutions (or negativity). We must see the gains to be made from good experiences and the lessons we can learn from mistakes.

Entrepreneur Spirit.

Entrepreneur spirit is the belief that a desired course of action to sell and exploit a solution is workable and achievable. This means a problem has been solved and has led to the creation of a vision. At this point the opportunity is mapped either informally in the heads of entrepreneurs or written down in an explicit form so that the idea can be shared and leveraged with others.

Entrepreneur Spirit is a case of a 'Can Do Attitude' meets available resources after considering the elements of a plan either formally or informally and deciding the necessary action is achievable. This means that the opportunity is viable having assessed the risk and considered the possible return on investment.

Entrepreneur Leap.

The 'entrepreneur leap' is the decision to take entrepreneur action, positive steps to achieve the entrepreneur vision.

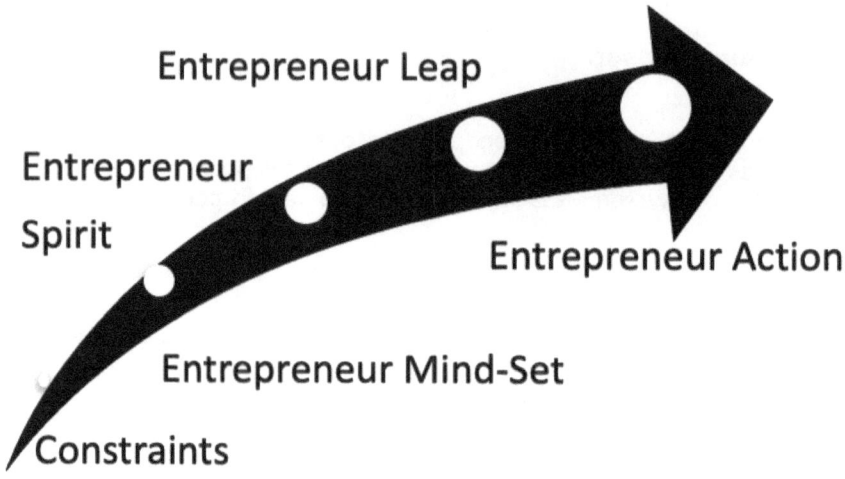

Oh great, I'm leaping today! We don't suddenly decide to make an entrepreneur leap and invest in a half-baked idea. The entrepreneur leap on the scale of things is a huge, deliberated decision and a conclusion reached after relevant thought depending on the size of the investment required and the potential for gains.

Entrepreneur Leap & Opportunity and Risk

To start an entrepreneur venture, at some point there must be a decision and the best decisions are as a result of asking great questions. The better your questions the more informative answers and the easier it is to reach a conclusion. But it's very difficult to influence the motivation to take a risk, only the decision-maker will know when they are satisfied that the opportunity is worth the risk. Teaching business skills in Universities has not been shown to have any effect on the entrepreneur leap unless they focus on innovation, process mapping and management systems. However, we can improve the chance of opportunity recognition, build confidence, develop entrepreneur skills and measure risks that will help analyse the situation in hand.

I found there are 2 schools of thought regarding the entrepreneur leap and these are money and ideas. Startups need access to finance, or the venture is doomed. However, in Australia a report suggests the barrier to the entrepreneur leap is more about a lack of ideas than a lack of funding. This doesn't make sense. I accept an entrepreneur with an idea needs finance to leap but arguably, an entrepreneur with money who needs an idea is not at the leap stage of entrepreneur start-up as they are still looking for constraints.

Anyway, a lack of ideas should never be a bar to entrepreneurship as there is certainly never a shortage of problems requiring solutions. But it seems opportunity recognition and innovation and funding are all issues concerning the entrepreneur leap.

The evidence suggests that while there are initiatives to support entrepreneurship these are still failing entrepreneurs because of a lack of focus on constraints, ideas, money or referents or a coming together of attitude, knowledge and skills that make the difference to leaping. This is true, especially for society's most deprived 10% where just 5% are self-employed.

Action, Leap, Spirit, Mindset

Entrepreneur & Environmental Balance

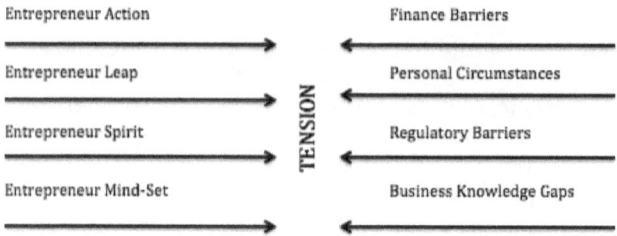

For every positive reason to drive the idea forward there will be another reason to hold–back the initiative until the time is right.

Entrepreneur Structures.

In the beginning there is no structure or start-up rules. The new entrepreneur owners develop the rules and procedures for new businesses using their skills as free thinkers, achievers and economic contributors. They are first innovators, adaptors and improvisers and these dynamics require loose structures. Secondly, entrepreneurs are motivators who move themselves, individuals, teams, suppliers, customers and suppliers toward some common goals that require low, medium and high structure as appropriate.

But new businesses are subject to the same high structure and rules as a mature organisation and are fettered by red tape and obligations to pay rent, rates, VAT and business registrations before they earn any money. Finally, an entrepreneur's success mostly relies on credibility and reputation, which requires high management structures and if the business is to scale then this too requires high structure. Therefore, in start-up there is a mix of low to high structure and this is relative to the speed of growth.

Entrepreneur Diversity

Change and Group Think

We have 'group think' in a group of people where the desire for harmony and conformity in the group results in an irrational or dysfunctional decision-making outcome. In entrepreneurship I have found the 'special person' argument is a group think subjectivity. This is because the wider evidence suggests entrepreneurs are normal people yet generally people believe the romantic notion that entrepreneurs are just born that way. This 'group think' extends to both teachers who teach children to get ready for jobs and those who support entrepreneurs but fail to 'reach out' to normal people and ask why they have not considered self-employment as a career path. Entrepreneurs are talented individuals who breakaway from the pack to provide economic benefit, they know they can change the world and enthusiastically and naturally encourage 'entrepreneurial group think' to help find ways to market themselves. However, initiatives supporting and driving entrepreneurs to leap is fettered by the 'group think' phenomenon of the 'special person entrepreneur.' Initiatives and their mentors who fail to reach out to entrepreneurs are failing the self-employed either in the absence or suitability because the 'group think' is that an entrepreneur with the next big idea will emerge. Arguably, more ideas will emerge if the 'group think' of an entrepreneur is applied to the initiatives and mentors, "Entrepreneurs will find a way" to improve the development of entrepreneurs. Developing entrepreneurs, "whether you think you can, or think you can't, you're right!"

A radical change in thinking in an entrepreneurial way is necessary to find a new approach and create both an abundance of entrepreneurs and intrapreneurs and drive the economy to higher levels of growth.

The benefits of developing entrepreneurs go far beyond the entrepreneur. Entrepreneurs provide, products, services, jobs, taxes and many more economic and social advantages on a local, national and global scale. Harbouring workable entrepreneurship programmes is money well spent, for governments. Reducing the unemployed both directly and indirectly through the need for entrepreneurs to employ workers, generating economic activity through supply chains and paying taxes.

More educational focus on entrepreneurship in a more dynamic manner may restore balance to a system that currently favours the training of employees. There is an economic demand for more entrepreneurial activity, however entrepreneurship is not for everyone, but everyone can benefit from entrepreneurial skills either directly or indirectly. It seems a travesty that university students are provided with cheap loans, but entrepreneurs struggle to find venture funding, there is certainly an imbalance in thinking here and who is more likely to repay the loan and fastest?

Entrepreneur Support.

Existing support for entrepreneurs fails in two ways. Not enough entrepreneurs make the entrepreneurial leap after attending business programmes and too many ventures fail in the first year of start-up. To improve entrepreneurship, we need to support entrepreneurs to leap and support entrepreneurs to survive and succeed.

Mentors

It's a two-way relationship. Entrepreneurs must use mentors as an asset. Entrepreneurs need mentors who are entrepreneurs themselves and see their role as contributing to the economy and the wider entrepreneur community. Entrepreneurs can teach the key entrepreneur skills and this knowledge should be captured, stored and made accessible.

Can we learn entrepreneurship from existing entrepreneurs? Considering that we are not born entrepreneurs, entrepreneurship is a lifelong and continuing learning experience. But it's up to individuals to make the link between the interpretation of events and experiences and entrepreneurship. Where the events and experiences are passed on by experienced entrepreneurs then maybe this is an effective means of dispersing knowledge about entrepreneur ventures. However, businesses are so different in the passage of time and disparity of industry and descriptive sentiment may not pass in the necessary key skills. Yes, every business is different, different products, different services, different problems and different people etc! How can an entrepreneur in an engineering venture learn from an entrepreneur from literature or the arts or catering? The industry and products may be different, but the key skills are the same! Key skills can be identified, captured, stored, made reusable and accessible and taught.

Funding

Before taking funding from anywhere ask lots of questions and consider your strategy and the drivers and barriers a financial burden or partners may bring to your business. While having a financial partner on board offering much needed cash injection and advice there are certain points to consider such as what funding is available and what are the consequences of involving borrowed funds in your venture.

Available funds include personal cash, family money, bank loans, short-term credit card usage, government funds and other funds such as venture capitalists or Angel investors.

Borrowing from family, banks, governments and credit cards offer investment without relinquishing power. However, you must pay repay the debts and consider the interest payments as part of your monthly cash flow liabilities.

When borrowing from investors, consider if you want to give up some power to investors and allow the business to maybe take a different direction or be influenced in decision-making by other appointees in senior level management positions. Consider the benefits of collaboration and think about the growth that may or may not be achieved and the costs. Then consider if the perceived growth is achievable on your own initiatives.

The level of success will rely on the good relations between the entrepreneur and the investor as a harmonious relationship where values are aligned is essential to drive business growth and besides, you will be spending a lot of time together over the next 5 to 10 years. The entrepreneur must be able to deliver on the plan whereas the investor must have a credible track record and be able to build a good working relationship based on a solid contractual arrangement and concise business plans.

Consider why the investor may be interested in your company, is it for the long-term business objectives or is it to make a quick financial turn-around on an investment or extract your business secrets! Consider how the investor's objectives may impact your business needs. The relationship should be transparent on how it will conclude. How will the arrangement end and how is the exit strategy triggered. We can avoid conflict and tension by building trusting relations that benefit from being open and transparent regarding partner terminations, buy back, quotations or trade sales and exit strategies that can result in venture compromise.

Internal & External Drivers

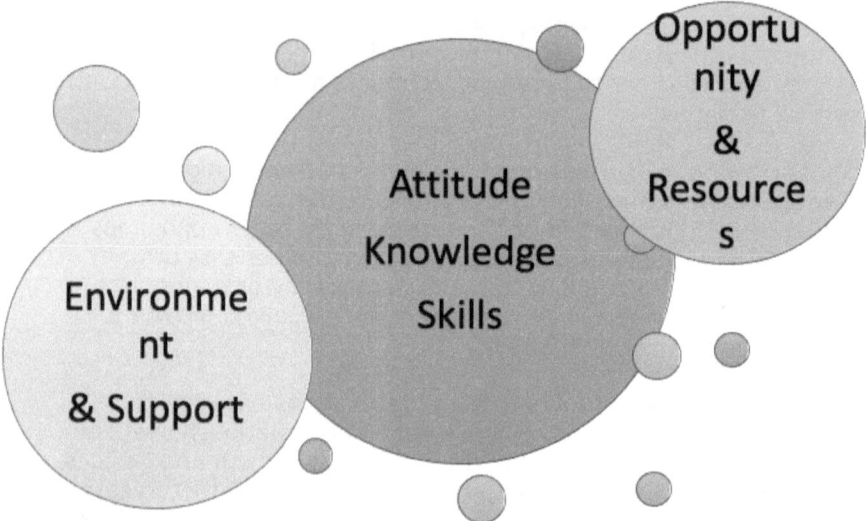

Internal

Attitude, Knowledge and Skills are personal to each and every entrepreneur. A positive attitude, industry and business knowledge and enhanced skills through practising the 'Art of Entrepreneurship.'

External

Opportunity, Resources, Environment and support are open to interpretation depending on each entrepreneur's Attitude, Knowledge and Skills.

For example: One entrepreneur may view a shortage of resources as a barrier whereas another may view the same situation as a challenge and therefore a driver.

The difference between missing an opportunity and spotting an opportunity is how an entrepreneur applies entrepreneur thinking, personal motivation, knowledge and experience to a constraint, available resources and the potential of exploitation.

Drivers Or Barriers?

The evidence in the UK suggests that people have great interest in setting up their own business and controlling their own financial futures. Many of these potential entrepreneurs believe that the success to any business depends on the start-up preparation and research of the market sector, especially in identifying there is a need for the product or services they intend to provide. However, the number of businesses started annually, arguably, does not reflect what people say and do, this is because of the barriers to entrepreneurship.

There are a number of barriers, and it is normally assumed the biggest reason for not pursuing an entrepreneur venture is the level of perceived risk. However, I found over 40 barriers to entrepreneurship, but I found just 4 Primary Barriers, and these are categorised as Finance, Business Knowledge, Personal Circumstances and Business Regulations. Arguably, if we want to improve entrepreneur thinking a great place to impact would be to identify, understand and remove these 4 primary barriers.

Barriers to Entrepreneurship:

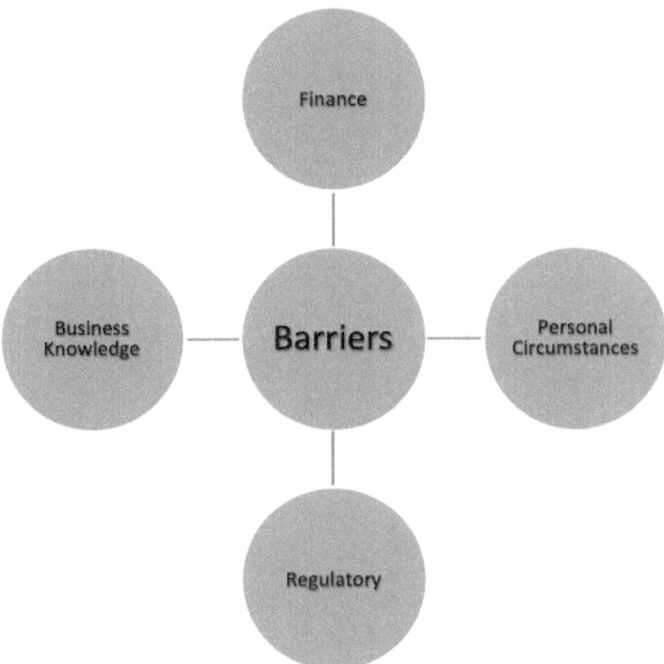

Business Knowledge:

Not having a business idea or being able to spot an opportunity.
Not knowing how to start a business.
Not having the necessary skills to start a business.
Not knowing where to go for help and advice.
Not knowing where to find business support
Not having any business relationships or networks
No sales experience, not knowing how to achieve sales
Not knowing how to convert customers to buyers
No experience of process, policies & procedures, systems and paperwork

Business Regulations:

Company formation & registration
Complex start-up regulations
Industry regulations
Health and safety
Employment law
National Insurance
Tax, Income, VAT & Corporation
Pensions

Finance:

Raising the finance for the business.
Finding investors for the business
Start-up funding
Identifying income streams early
Generating cash flow
Margins, achieving the correct sales v cost ratio
Business Costs, materials, cost of sales, employees, utilities
Cost of premises, flexibility and availability
Fear the business may fail
Fear of debt

Personal Circumstances:

Timing
No one understands
Lack of confidence
Income insecurity
Losing the security of your current job.
Losing the income from your current job.
Good promotional prospects in your current job.
Loneliness
Childcare
Sickness & Long-term illness

Barriers and the 'Entrepreneur Leap'

Before making a decision to start a new venture entrepreneurs must consider their own competencies against the known barriers to success. There are 4 primary barriers business knowledge, business regulations, finance and personal circumstances. Entrepreneurs considering leaping must be confident of their capabilities to overcome barriers to success to reduce business risk. Therefore, the probability of venture success is planned informally or formally before any action is taken and the level of planning reduces uncertainty and exposes risks. Once entrepreneurs are confident of their own capabilities to achieve their vision and plan there is an increased probability of an entrepreneur leap. Venture success and survival is more probable where risks are transparent and knowledge gaps, skills and capabilities are adjusted to meet venture demands.

Entrepreneur action noticeably starts with the entrepreneur leap where resources are motivated in pursuit of the vision. Arguably, at this point barriers have been considered and accepted or strategies are to be designed to ensure barriers do not prevent venture success. For example, a knowledge gap can be overcome through advice or education, but government regulations must be adhered to, and strategies must be put in place that ensures the venture does not fall foul of its responsibilities.

What really makes a difference to entrepreneurs and start-up decisions include:

1.   A great idea that is worth risking investment.
2.   The ability to navigate around barriers.
3.   The money to start and drive the vision and overcome barriers.
4.   Motivation not to be deterred by obstacles such as barriers.

Therefore, the entrepreneur leap is a result of an entrepreneur mind-set converging with entrepreneur spirit. This means having identified a problem and solution the entrepreneur is in no doubt they can achieve the vision.

Business Knowledge

In any human activity we need to either have the knowledge or know how to find the necessary information to be able to undertake the venture successfully. Otherwise, we are taking an enormous risk. Entrepreneur training can start with business knowledge but should include research skills, industry knowledge and the power of networks. Probably most importantly sales training too. I once asked a business graduate why businesses fail, and the response was that it was down to poor planning. In fact, most businesses were found to fail (47%) because there was no identified market need for the product or service. If there is no need there are no sales, and the venture will quickly run out of cash. Business knowledge is important, but it is entrepreneur knowledge that is useful in a start-up. Entrepreneur training must focus on the ability to seek out constraints and opportunity and develop an entrepreneur mind-set that helps to find new ways of providing solutions. Then focus on a market gap analysis to identify the need for the solution you are proposing and if in doubt test the market first.

Business is a fairly simple process. We identify a need, provide a solution, and develop and manufacture the product or services. Deliver the product and get paid.

Let's look at Google as an example. The identified problem was the quality of results in a search engine. This transpired to be a maths problem and when solved became a code. The code is the product for the Google search engine. Google then gave the search engine away so that you and I can search for free and created a network of Google users. Then Google introduced advertisers who paid to advertise on the network. Google is able to leverage its systems to grow its business on a global scale and generate $billions. Every business can grow like Google, every business has the same type of capability to recognise and understand what really drives their business is the same processes. While working for a firm of intellectual capital accountants we found that most businesses have around 87 processes, that's it! Our job is to map these processes in order to grow as this enables replication, leverage and economies of scale.

There is a vast void between running a business and being an entrepreneur and the difference is normally one of scale. For example, I may be a self-employed window cleaner, or I can provide the systems to deliver professional cleaning across the capital city. The disparity between the processes will be found to be mostly a difference in scale of systems, processes and procedures but essentially the product or service is the same.

Another example is Uber, it's a taxi business no different to any other but brought together through technology processes that generates $billions.

Wider Barriers & Business Knowledge

Hiring new people and training them to a regulatory or industry standard is costly and that's if you can find the right people. When we start a business, we may not think of our partners as internal barriers however, people acting outside their contracts can be detrimental to the business and its owners. Internal barriers include key workers leaving with company secrets (whistleblowers) or cultural change from new CEO's (Apple & Steve Jobs), or shareholders requiring reduced emphasis on employee retention and greater emphasis on cost reduction. All of these can affect the business and its credibility to satisfy customers and even the ability to act entrepreneurially.

Business Knowledge

Business Knowledge Barriers	
Business Knowledge	**Entrepreneur**
No business idea	Look for Constraints / GROWTH
Unable to spot an opportunity	Provide solutions that take away pain
No business start-up skills	Simply start
Not knowing where to find help/advice	The government will help / networks
Not knowing where to find support	Internet / Join a trade organisation
Not having any business relationships	Join business network groups
Unaware of industry networks	Internet search
No sales experience	PAIDBACK in this book
Not knowing how to achieve sales	Performance management
Not knowing how to convert customers	Ask for the order
Not knowing how to price products	Consider costs v price people will pay
No experience of process, policies & procedures, systems, and paperwork	Map your activities, there will be less than 100 processes

Finally, a nations growth is directly related to investment in entrepreneurial competencies and ability to nurture young people to develop entrepreneur skills. While long-term unemployment is directly related to habitually mismanaging youths and failing to develop a belief in their ability to succeed. Therefore, developing economic activity depends on investment in entrepreneurship, apprenticeships for under 21's, investment in vocational qualifications for under 21's or investment in higher education.

The cost of long-term unemployment can be significantly reduced by increased focus on providing a choice for every under 21 year old to:

Continue education or   Start a business or Learn a trade, profession or vocation.

Regulatory

Government regulations put people off the entrepreneurial leap. If ever there is a barrier to start-up this, is it. People fear the unknown liabilities that are a result of governments demanding their share of entrepreneurial activity while also preventing entrepreneurial activity. It's a double-edged regulatory sword. However, entrepreneurs must consider regulatory barriers as these can both assist the development of the business by improving quality standards or fetter growth through the cost of compliance. Compliance includes the cost of industry standards, product liability, health and safety and licenses and taxation. It is prudent to factor into business plans regulatory costs as you may discover regulatory liabilities and due dates may be a severe handicap on achieving financial plans and think how entrepreneurs may legally avoid regulations.

Regulations impose high structure on entrepreneurs and when structure cannot be overcome this acts as a barrier to growth and venture success, therefore, entrepreneurs must identify regulations, liabilities and their effect on the business and in particular effects on financial plans then design unique ways to meet liabilities or circumnavigate the effects on the business.

When at planning stages, identify structures that promote free flowing ideas and venture development. Government should aim to remove prohibitive structures and regulations in favour of cost neutral entrepreneur development structures. There should be time to recognise diversity and drive entrepreneur change. This also requires an active programme of change amongst restrictive entrepreneur support programmes and their mentors who may prefer regulatory and legal compliance over business efficacy. This is a difficult scale to balance and getting this wrong can mean legal implications or an overburdened regulatory financial liability. Either way a startup is unlikely to survive due to so much bureaucracy that fetters entrepreneur thinking.

Regulations

Regulatory Barriers	
Regulations	**Entrepreneur**
Company Formation	Take legal advice
Registration	Register with HMRC
Complex start-up regulations	The government will help
Industry regulations	Join the trade organisation
Health and safety	Mostly common sense / take advice
Employment law	HR remote / lots of companies to help
National Insurance, Income Tax	Leave for HR company
Corporation Tax	Accountants / Only if you have profits
Vat	Check HMRC thresholds
Pensions	Stakeholder Pensions apply

Finance

Without the money to start the business it is unlikely even the best ideas will lead to a startup venture no matter how committed or motivated you are. The 'Entrepreneur leap' requires access to support and finance or capital investment. There are a variety of ways to fund a business such as personal savings, inheritance, windfalls, redundancy payments, credit cards, bank loans, partners, venture capitalists and Angel Investors. Access to startup capital will really come down to the ability of the business idea to make enough profit to repay the loans. Entrepreneurs must consider the financial barriers to the business and highlight the risks in a business plan that financial investors will be making and the expected return on investment. This means highlighting why you need the money and exactly what you will do with it and the effect this will have on growing the business.

Entrepreneurs must overcome the financial barriers and start up financial decisions will determine the future success or failure of the venture as heavy borrowing can mean the business struggling to meet liabilities where sales are below forecast, or cash flow is unpredictable. Running out of cash is a sure way to business failure therefore, considering worse case scenarios and thinking of contingencies is a good way to assess the probability of success.

Most businesses fail because there is no market need for the product or service. Early steps should be, to identify the market and test your product. Be prepared to change your product or service following testing and consider your solution against your competitor's offer and the strategies competitors may take to counter your market entry. If you find you need to change your product or services to meet testing results, then make sure you also update your business plan to represent the product or service changes amend the financial plans too.

The financial business plan must provide comprehensive details of how this business will take away pain or provide pleasure and why people will pay you for your solution. The true costs must be explicit and accompanied by financial assessments and forecasts such as:

Profit and loss account and Balance Sheet

- Spending plan
- Budget constraints analysis
- Contingency plans
- Cash flow forecast
- Identified income streams
- Growth plan
- Financial Forum
- Cost Control

Business plans can be informal, but the best ones are a written document clearly outlining the business and its objectives, strategies, tactics, sales, marketing, and financial information. If you are trying to secure finance, then a business plan is the best way to represent your business. There are many business plan templates available online or from banks and government agencies and even organisations helping to complete plans or to help find the finance from government grant schemes. However, large, detailed documents may be required for finance investment, your presentation to investors must be a maximum of 10 slides or even 7 slides. (Think 7 points, 7 slides. 7 minutes).

Financial Planning Model

Profit and Loss Account

A profit and loss account provides a breakdown of the liabilities and shows what you need money for and also how much money you will make from the business activities. Research your business needs, consider the tools and machinery you need and obtain quotes. What else will you need, premises, staff, utilities etc. Get quotes for expenditure and compare liabilities against expected sales and exactly what marketing you will need to do to acquire the customers to provide the sales. You must demonstrate how investors can expect a return on their investment and how and when you think profit margins will ensure profits.

Spending Plan

Consider when you will need to purchase business items, consider deposits and lead times and contractual obligations and think about how these will impact sales orders. Machinery must not be left idle as it costs money if its unused, but we must ensure essential means of production are delivered on time and doesn't prevent fulfilling generated sales obligations. Then as the business grows how you will change work processes to meet sales demands and the key performance indicators you will use to measure sales performance and highlight favourable trends and unfavourable deviances. Spend other people's money wisely, save costs where possible and resist your personal financial being at the cost of investors, its unethical, apart from this when you need help to grow a carefully managed venture is more likely to have sympathetic lenders.

Cash Flow Forecast

Think about the activity in your business, if you can show investors when the money is expected this can increase interest in your business. When will you start selling to customers, how much will you need to outlay to get the products moving and when will the first invoices be paid. What will you need to do to break even? If possible, show the results from product testing, revenues made, advance orders and proof of any contracts you have agreed. Include all your costs and income streams and be brutally honest, as everything, sales and costs, must add up. You must include your own wages here, exactly what you need to take from the business to live on and include personal liabilities as well such as mortgage or car loans as this demonstrates you are able to manage your debts. Then who will you have to pay and what order you will consider paying the liabilities. Are you able to negotiate discounted supply costs for early payment that will positively complement cash-flow liabilities? Demonstrate a clear understanding of how the business receivables and liabilities will be managed and controlled.

Budget Constraints Analysis

Also consider the things we must pay to keep the business running such as lawyers and accountants, insurance, Health & Safety, maintenance contracts and business liabilities such as taxes and VAT. How will these liability constraints impact cash-flow if something unexpectedly happens and what action can we take to stay ahead of the game and not lose sales or customers. At what point we will need to hire extra employees and who will they be, how much will we pay and under what terms. Hire slowly but fire fast. Then think of how we can use technology to keep labour costs low and return on investment high.

Contingency Plans

Not all business ventures work out, so also consider the action you will take and when if the business fails. How will you know its failing? What will you do? How will you pay creditors and stay out of debt. Be aware of market influences, changes in customer trends and economic fluctuations such as recession and how we will survive if the proverbial falls on us.

Identified Income Streams

Demonstrate that you have thought about possible income streams. For example, if you are a business selling slices of cakes maybe you can sell cakes, open a coffee shop, upgrade to quality cupcakes, sell birthday cakes and cakes for special occasions. Then sell other catering businesses your ingredients such as flour and sugar. Maybe you can diversify into delivering your cakes and delivering for other shops at the same time. Once you have established the business you could expand the number of shops, invite a franchise opportunity, buy properties and rent parts to private tenants or other businesses.

Growth plan

Securing loans or investment funding is just the start. Once we have secured funding on the idea the business moves to selling hard products or services. Entrepreneurs can help themselves secure the funding by demonstrating how the business will use initial investment to drive sales of real products and support long-term growth. A growth plan would take into account how the business will achieve economies of scale and leverage resources and consider the economic up-turns and downturns too. Early in the venture it is prudent to consider mapping the business processes to expand the business model as an identical unit that can be sited in other parts of the country or even across the world. Then we need to think about the money, how do we grow money, hedge resources, and leverage cash through investment in property or other businesses and moving liquid funds to protective structures such as legal trusts. A 'cash-rich' business is more likely to grow even in a recession, however, a business that exists on debt is more likely to become a statistic of failure.

Financial Forum

Manage the business money smartly. Have meetings where spending is accountable and transparent, and ideas can be raised. Have many means of communication from meetings, briefings, knowledge forums, GROWTH meetings, grapevines or happy notice boards where anyone can write praise, solution or a grievance. Keep decision makers in the loop and inventory low. React to low productivity quickly and ensure the business remains competitive. Consider where cost savings are possible, reduce errors, minimise wastage and leakage and streamline financial systems through automation and minimise compliance risk. Then ask what else can we do?

Cost Control

Identify partners that deliver complementary and cost saving outsourcing such as payroll, HR, Health & Safety. Reduce paper, use software suppliers or cloud computing software, focus on saving costs on supply chain networks, encourage the use of personal devices for work tasks.

Finance

Finance & Barriers	
Finance	**Entrepreneur**
Raising the finance for the business.	Gifts, inheritance, re-mortgage
Finding investors for the business	Banks, Venture Capitalists, Angels
Start-up funding	Personal, family, credit, loans
Identifying income streams	How can we generate early income
Generating cash flow	Invoice promptly
Achieving the correct sales v cost ratio	Costs & price customers will pay
Setting Profit Margins	Mark up to achieve the set profit
Business Costs, materials	All physical assets
Total Cost of Sales	Record all costs tangible & intangible
Employees	As and when needed
Utilities	Mandatory liabilities
Fear the business may fail	Business Plans / Assess risk
Fear of debt	Control Costs

Note on Student Debt & Start up:

Does student debt provide entrepreneurs that increase economic activity? Student debt probably prevents entrepreneurship, as college graduates with debt are less likely to borrow more money to finance a business venture. Therefore, there is less possibility of students investing in entrepreneurial ventures that promote a work ethic unemployment and state benefits while creating jobs and raising taxes.

Personal Circumstances

Where we are personally is subjective to each and every entrepreneur. This is the difficult area to assess and improve as we are in danger of reverting to personality traits and behavioural characteristics, and this is a concern for pragmatists as Personality and Psychological tests have been found to have absolutely no bearing in who will become future entrepreneurs. In any event though interesting and considered by some important we want to go beyond the personality boundaries and focus on personal circumstances. Specifically, we are concerned with the development of entrepreneur thinking as a driver rather than thinking of personal circumstances as a barrier that fetters entrepreneur action.

Thus, identifying common barriers amongst people's personal circumstances can help identify issues we can focus resources on to influence entrepreneur development. We found 13 barriers under personal circumstances.

Overcoming these barriers requires simple solutions such as building confidence and education in entrepreneurship, business knowledge and business and industry regulations. This requires a supportive and nurturing entrepreneur culture to build confidence and belief in capabilities to take action and succeed. Nurturing the entrepreneur spirit is a means of developing a 'can do' attitude and an entrepreneur mindset where people seek out opportunity.

Arguably, personal circumstances can be eliminated or designed to have a negative impact through nurturing and training, business knowledge is achievable through courses and work experience, finance can be generated both internally and externally and Business Regulations can be relaxed and eliminated for new businesses up to a nominal turnover threshold e.g., £100k. Simple cost neutral solutions.

Thereafter, it's a case of considering yourself ready and able to take on the challenge of being self-employed, earning your own money, paying liabilities and employing others. But don't procrastinate. Often in a new entrepreneur venture the speed of a start-up means time becomes both a referent and a barrier as opportunity for advancement replaces the old product. Time influences the dynamic activity that takes place to improvise, adapt and imitate where necessary to drive a new product to market. The creative destruction of old ways in replace of new systems and procedures is influenced by timing ahead of competitors who will be fast on your heels as you try to capture market share. As a new entrepreneur you enter a lion's den where it's a case of eat or be eaten. Think about timing and your product suitability for launching in your decided market at this particular point in time.

Then consider the advantages and disadvantages of being an entrepreneur against your present personal circumstances.

Personal Circumstances

Personal Circumstances - Pros & Cons	
Personal Circumstances	**Entrepreneur**
Losing job security	Higher levels of job satisfaction
Income insecurity	Unlimited earning potential
No-one understands	Huge business support network in UK
Good promotional prospects at work	You will be CEO
Less control over daily work / life	Total control of daily agenda
Losing regular income	Work as much or as little as you want
Loneliness	Employ team & talk to customers
Childcare	Childcare
Sickness and long-term illness	Insurance and high levels of energy
Worried about timing	Simply leap and find out

Timing

Timing is influenced by 'referents' personal to the entrepreneur's unique perceptions. This means the coming together of attitude, knowledge, skills, and opportunity, resources and environment. Timing influences the availability of resources both at the time the opportunity is presented and after the initial research and development analysis is concluded. The resources that were initially available such as for example, the availability of people or money may have changed for the better or worse. Entrepreneurs must think about how the opportunity can be exploited using whatever resources are at hand, this means improvising by using something that was not meant for the purpose it may now be used, adapting something to satisfy the need or innovating something entirely new to provide the solution. Making the entrepreneurial leap and creating, adapting or improvising new products or services will mean thinking outside of the box to control costs, acquire resources, build organisational culture, define boundaries to provide exploitable solutions.

In this type of dynamic environment, the entrepreneur is unbounded, entrepreneurs make the rules, develop processes and systems that will leverage available resources and eventually scale the business. Start-ups are, therefore, flexible, loose structures with the ability to change direction fast based on internal or external dynamics. Entrepreneurs who are willing to go beyond the normal industry boundaries are taking risks that must be considered if a satisfactory outcome is to be achieved. This also requires a culture of rule breaking that some people may be unwilling to adopt in search of improvisational solutions.
However, recognised opportunities are time-bound and procrastination can leave the door open for your competitors to steal market share that will never be recovered. Entrepreneurs learn to think to take action, simply take a first step or just do it are phrases often heard around start-up decisions. Time wasting will impede the decision to act entrepreneurially and take advantage of a perceived opportunity.

Entrepreneurs are often more successful the second time or third time and arguably this is because of the lessons learned from earlier procedural mistakes. However, learning by doing is an expensive way to learn and it must be considered more prudent to learn about the many systematic human and business processes prior to the entrepreneur leap, this will save time and resources and help lead to faster return on investment and a higher probability of venture survival. This is because where an event is happening over and over again, we are able to develop a process either formally in systems or informally as know-how.

This may explain a rise in experienced 'grey entrepreneurs' found in a 2004 study where experience and know-how meet opportunity. When the event comes around again there is a higher chance the opportunity may be grasped, and a start-up ensue. In trying to develop entrepreneur thinking it is important to consider the elements that are routine compared to the happenings that are variable and unpredictable in order to get the business off the ground fast, developing income streams and much needed cash-flow.

Positive or Negative Capital in our Barriers and Drivers: Motivators?

Barriers and Drivers		
Human Capital	**Structural Capital**	**Network Capital**
People	Results	Rewards
Age	Finance, Tax,	No Income
Health	Advice	Income insecurity
Confidence	Start-up funding	Distribution
Loneliness	Regulations	Channels
No Ideas	Premises	Employees
Illness	Procedures	Customers
Vision Alignment	Processes, Systems	Suppliers
Fear of Failure	Cost Control	Family
Innovation	Securing assets	Childcare
	(in/tangible)	Protection
	Motivation	

Identifying and categorising the barriers to entrepreneurship is one way of finding the means to overcome procrastination.

Barriers to Entrepreneurship Matrix

Barriers to Entrepreneurship	
Finance	**Business Knowledge**
Raising the finance for the business. **Finding investors for the business** **Start-up funding** **Identifying income streams early** **Generating cash flow** **Setting Profit Margins** **Achieving the correct sales v cost ratio** **Business Costs, materials, cost of sales, employees, utilities** **Cost of premises, flexibility and availability** **Fear the business may fail** **Fear of debt**	No business idea Unable to spot an opportunity. No business start-up skills Not knowing where to find help/advice Not knowing where to find support Not having any business relationships Unaware of industry networks No sales experience, Not knowing how to achieve sales Not knowing how to convert customers Not knowing how to price products No experience of process, policies & procedures, systems and paperwork
Personal Circumstances	**Business Regulations**
Timing (You will know) **No-one understands** **Lack of confidence** **Income insecurity** **Losing the security of your current job.** **Losing your employment income** **Good promotional prospects at work** **Loneliness** **Childcare** **Sickness and Long-term illness**	Company formation & registration Complex start-up regulations Industry regulations Health and safety Employment law National Insurance Corporation Tax Income Tax Vat Pensions

7 reasons entrepreneur barriers exist.

1.   **Culture.** Some countries are very good at turning out entrepreneurs, other countries invest in turning out entrepreneurs and other countries have poor entrepreneur records. For example, the USA is very good at nurturing entrepreneurs and believing that as people they can achieve their dreams. Countries such as India turn out entrepreneurs simply because of extreme circumstances of poverty. The UK and Australia invest in entrepreneur programmes but don't really understand if its ideas or money that drives entrepreneurship and start-up ventures are below countries like USA or India. Countries like Spain and Portugal turn out much lower entrepreneur ventures in comparison. The difference between these entrepreneur cultures varies enormously but common factors include the belief of achievement, the need to achieve and finance as a driver. Therefore, referents that make a difference in these circumstances are the nurturing of ability to seek out problems, developing the belief that we can find a way to solve problems and achieve results and providing or depriving of finance as a driver. So, if we really want to change a generation, we must focus on culture such as nurturing children and young people to think and act entrepreneurially and then supporting them.

2.   **Mindset.** Progress means change and change is a result of people being dissatisfied with the status quo. However, conformity is taught to children. But entrepreneurs are known to seek out constraints and find solutions to problems they can exploit. This means continuous change where some people prefer the status quo, and this creates tension. Therefore, an entrepreneur mindset drives progress as people seek out constraints that can increase the probability of entrepreneur ventures.

3.   **Spirit.** Give the mind a problem and it will find a way to solve it, then add scale and this is entrepreneur spirit and big picture thinking and requires nurturing.

4.   **Leap.** The motivation to weigh up the odds of success and take a risk requires confidence and know-how of how to uncover uncertainties and make risks known. Entrepreneurs will not risk investment unless there is a high probability of return and measurement requires high levels of analysis.

5.   **Structures**. Entrepreneurs are free thinkers, achievers and economic contributors, they are also innovators, adaptors and improvisers and these dynamics require loose structures. However, both known and unknown regulatory barriers that include, high regulatory structures such as industry regulations and government legal requirements fetter entrepreneur creativity.

6.   **Change and group think.** A recent UK study demonstrates a group think phenomenon where entrepreneur problems remain the same because the same solutions are proposed that are proven to not make a difference. This results in dysfunctional support. Keep doing the same things and you'll get the same results. There's nothing new, however, nothing new is required as the people proposing entrepreneur change are not believers in new and diverse approaches. This is classic equilibrium theory.

7.   **Support.** Existing support is sporadic and is short-term with poor success rates reflected in the high number of businesses that fail in the first year.

The 7 Social Reasons for Entrepreneur Barriers

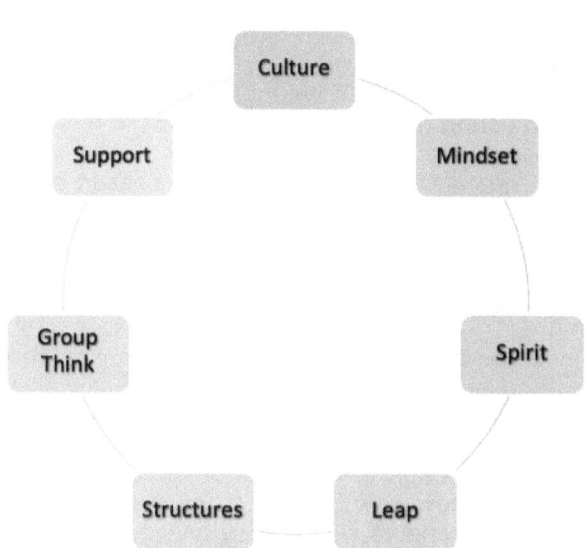

The 4 Strategic Barriers to Entrepreneurship

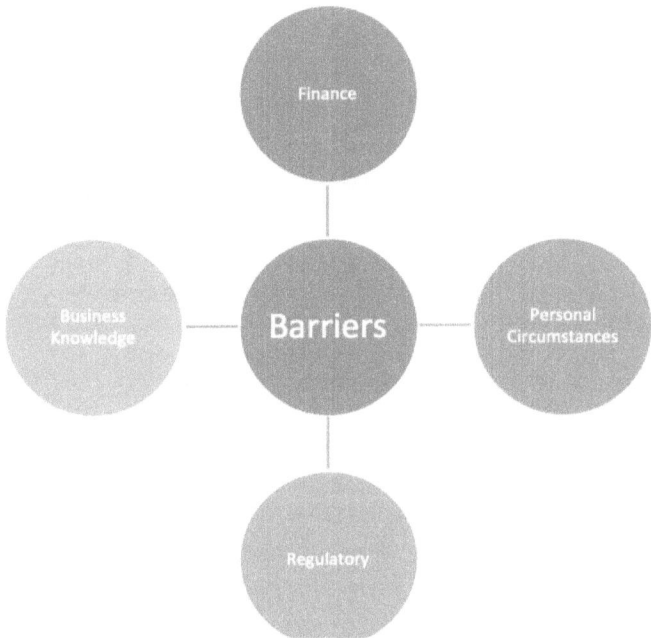

Overcoming the 4 Barriers to Entrepreneurship

We found 4 barriers to entrepreneurship.

- Personal Circumstances
- Finance
- Business Knowledge
- Regulatory

To overcome the 4 barriers to entrepreneurship we must address the 7 social reasons responsible for the entrepreneur barriers.

1. Entrepreneur Culture
2. Entrepreneur Mindset
3. Entrepreneur Spirit
4. Entrepreneur Leap
5. Entrepreneur Structures
6. Entrepreneur Diversity / Group Think
7. Entrepreneur Support

In 2016 a UK study found that despite many initiatives to help entrepreneurs obstacles to enterprise still exist and therefore, I question the effectiveness of initiatives in tackling the 7 social reasons for entrepreneur barriers. However, the report does provide recommendations to improve future entrepreneur activity but surprisingly the recommendations have been recommended and tested before and have not substantially increased entrepreneur activity.

There are 5 key issues identified in the study:

1. Mentors to be found amongst existing self-employed
2. Existing funding should be improved
3. Provide improved access to start-up loans
4. Focus on education for the next generation
5. Encourage banks to lend more to start-ups

Some critics argue that while everything here is useful, it's all been done before. Then my question is why are we still at the same point, same problems, same recommendations and same failings? The new recommendations must at least overcome the 4 barriers Personal Circumstances, Finance, Business Knowledge and Regulatory, if entrepreneurs are going to be supported to improve their economic contribution. Only 2 (at a stretch 3) of the 4 barriers can be identified from the research findings and these are business education and finance (maybe regulatory dependent on mentor experience). Clearly, the key issues do not provide an adequate solution to removing the reasons for the barriers to entrepreneurship and neither are all these barriers identified. I would extend this reasoning to specific areas and argue that recommendations must build confidence through improving personal circumstances, provide knowledge of business processes, develop finance skills and access to finance and explain, advise and reduce the regulatory burden on new businesses.

When we keep doing the same things to fix a problem, we will get the same results. Nothing new, means nothing will change. What is needed is a new approach that is holistic in nature and taking into account past failings and the management methods employed to make a difference and keep the good parts but eliminate and replace the parts that are ineffective. Then improve entrepreneurship with modern theories that will have a positive effect on reducing the 7 social reasons that obstruct enterprise.

So, what we need to do to boost entrepreneur thinking is to address the 7 social reasons that cause the barriers to entrepreneurship. Building confidence, business knowledge and access to finance will also help reduce the barriers. Finally, the government must examine how a reduction on regulations for new businesses can have a positive effect on developing young entrepreneurs to consider entrepreneurship as a career choice but also how this can contribute to the social and economic benefit of the nation through encouraging entrepreneur thinking.

Overcoming Barriers to Entrepreneurship

The 5 Key Skills (Necessary to Overcome Barriers)

The 5 key skills are comprised of 4 non-financial skills plus the expected one financial skill. The 4 key skills (non-financial) of entrepreneurship, are organising, inventing, leading and managing. Clearly these are special skills and rarely found in an inexperienced person, these skills require life experience, work experience, people and motivation, some natural characteristics and some nurture plus formal and informal education that make a well-rounded individual or team.

Key Skills:

Coordinating
Inventing
Leading
Managing
And Finance

Therefore, entrepreneur support should focus on these 5 key skills:

1. Coordinators spot an opportunity and gather the necessary resources
2. Inventors, discovering ideas, developing ways to innovate, adapt and improvise and provide value making solutions
3. Leaders, take action, achieve results and make a profit
4. Managers, measure and consider risks, networks, relations and value
5. Capital management and the effects of financial risks and strategies.

Every entrepreneur learns these skills to survive through work or life experience, which may or may not include education. This may be a more difficult means of learning a craft compared with some students who crash revision to pass exams. However, this may be the only means by which an entrepreneur can learn their craft where formal learning does not provide instruction in how to find ideas, achieve results or manage value or financial Capital. For many entrepreneurs there is no entrepreneur handbook, and the craft is a case of self-discovery, self-learning and self-motivation.

The Internet is a great resource for entrepreneurs who can find information at a click of a button about the many obscure and unique business opportunities they discover or develop. Knowledge creates unprecedented opportunity to develop a young person's entrepreneurial mindset and raises the probability of amazing entrepreneurial technological advances. However, to increase entrepreneur activity adding some structure will help provide much needed entrepreneur support. Improving entrepreneur support, providing information regarding the skill set and developing easily accessible, and achievable mastery may take time. But there is a double benefit of educating entrepreneurs. Where there are trained and potential entrepreneurs who are employed this provides an entrepreneurial workforce where the skills are put to work for employers. This can help provide inimitable competitive advantage and contribute to business drivers and the economy in yet unperceived entrepreneurial ways.

Entrepreneur Value Drivers

Opportunity recognition, Discovering solutions, Delivering results
Protecting rewards, And Finance

Entrepreneur Value Drivers		
Coordinator	ORGANISE	Opportunity Resource Growth Achievement Niche or Not Improvise Stress Tolerant Exploitation
Inventor	GROWTH	Goals Reality Options Who Will Win When Tracking Help
Leader	PAIDBACK	Planning Action Intention, Interest, Ingenuity Desire Benefits & Features Advantages Connection, Cheque & Check
Manager	PROTECT	Process Risk, Reporting, Relations Operations Tactics Employees Capital Time
Finance	CASH	Capital Assessment Streams Hedge

Entrepreneur Resources (Roles Tools and Drivers)

The entrepreneur resources are innovation, adaptation and improvisation, whatever is around them, whatever is to hand and whoever is skilled and available. This is called 'bricolage'.

Roles

The roles in entrepreneurship are of Coordinator, Inventor, Leader Manager and the role of Finance. Once roles are identified we can build courses around these roles that will provide influences for future entrepreneurs. Potential entrepreneurs can identify knowledge gaps, build their own skills or ensure the skills of an entrepreneur team meet the criteria for team balance.

Tools

The tools we have identified are the entrepreneur models in the form of the mnemonics ORGANISE, GROWTH, PAIDBACK, PROTECT & CASH. Applying these tools in the entrepreneur venture help focus the mind on the dominant role and the delivery of specific solutions that help develop entrepreneur thinking.

Tasks

ORGANISE to make order from chaos and identify constraints.
GROWTH helps find innovative ways that improve the current state.
PAIDBACK is a strategy to lead and motivate people to move toward new goals.
PROTECT ensures venture survival through risk management.
CASH is a structure to leverage financial resources and drive profit generation.

Types of Entrepreneur

There are two types of entrepreneur Solus and Social. The Solus Entrepreneur is motivated by the financial rewards of effort. The Social Entrepreneur is motivated uppermost by the solutions that benefit mankind and as a result a financial profit is derived but this is not the biggest motivational driver.

Motivations
Personal physiological needs or Solutions that benefit mankind

Drivers
Money is the primary driver.

Barriers to Entrepreneurship

Personal Circumstances
Finance
Regulatory
Business Knowledge

The 7 Social Reasons Failing Entrepreneurs

Overcoming the 4 barriers to entrepreneurship requires attention to the 7 social reasons that are failing entrepreneur development.

Entrepreneur Culture
A focus on encouraging children to believe in their ability, to build confidence, knowledge and entrepreneurial skills and belief by parents, schools, colleges.

Entrepreneur Mindset
Developing a mindset that questions the status quo. Why do we do things this way and encourage people to ask, 'is there a better way'.

Entrepreneur Spirit
A 'can do attitude' where we have assessed the possibility of developing people, entrepreneurs, a product or service and found a way forward. It's not a case of sheer bloody mindedness (although sometimes this may help) but a risk assessed opportunity to drive solutions that make a profit.

Entrepreneur Leap
Entrepreneurs are at a point where entrepreneur action is the next logical step. There is a solution, resources and know-how in place that will make a return on investment, and this is fully believed.

Entrepreneur Structures
Understanding the loose structures required for entrepreneur ventures to develop and finding ways to meet liabilities or to avoid them is often key to venture survival and financial success.

Entrepreneur Diversity / Group Think
Entrepreneurs are as diverse as the many industries and businesses they represent. Therefore, a one shoe fits all is impossible and group think should be avoided. However, there are many positive similarities in the skills of people involved in entrepreneur decision-making and we must focus on these identifiable skills to influence entrepreneur growth. Focus on where we can make a difference.

Entrepreneur Support
Support must focus on the 4 specific barriers and the reduction of the effects of the 7 social reasons failing entrepreneurs and think more long-term.

Where Are We Now?

Through my research I've found that some people believe entrepreneurs are born while other people prefer a scientific approach based on the making of an entrepreneur. There's no easy to answer to people's opinions about the born or made argument but the intelligent answer is to conclude that irrespective what we believe we can discover the ingredients of entrepreneur action and develop ways to influence entrepreneur development.

Barriers still exist and we struggle to identify these barriers and categorise them into meaningful groups that can be targeted for improvement with effective strategies.

There are wider issues regarding the development of entrepreneur education and training, and these remain in the social development of people predominantly the unhealthy 'group think' toward the 'special person theory'. Barriers such as business knowledge, business regulations and confidence are not really barriers at all. All of these perceived barriers may be overcome through specific education programmes that build know-how and confidence and entrepreneurial belief. I found the root causes preventing the education of entrepreneurs is locked in tri-fold handcuffs.

1. Traditional education focuses on preparing people for jobs
2. The content of entrepreneur programmes has little success in turning out start-up ventures
3. Support groups, because of 'group think' are reluctant to strategic change

The real barrier to entrepreneurship is not knowing how to develop the 5 entrepreneur skills that produce ideas, solutions and results and venture survival and finding the money to finance self-employment and entrepreneurship.

While Mentors is a useful asset for an entrepreneur a high number of business failures in the first year suggests change is need amongst mentors. The 'ad hoc' approach of everyone being a mentor because they are self-employed is cost intensive, unknown territory and unworkable. New entrepreneurs need specific help to ensure at least the top 5 reasons for business failure are covered in a strategic mentoring approach.

In reality funding is inadequate, and my assumption is that, funding entrepreneurship and removing regulatory barriers will provide a cost-neutral solution as entrepreneurs create jobs and other social benefits. Therefore, encouraging entrepreneurship as a way of life will reduce the burden on the state to provide jobs or social welfare benefits. Also, entrepreneur type courses will make people more ready for work including employers who will benefit from intrapreneurial type workers that can provide insight into new and better ways of providing solutions. Thus, entrepreneur funding is a double-edged sword for industry and the economy.

Focus on Entrepreneur Needs

Apart from money, an entrepreneur needs an attitude that seeks out constraints that require solutions, the knowledge and competencies to turn solutions into exploitable opportunity and the skills to make goals a reality. This requires the ability to spot an opportunity, to research and analyse the risks and the probability of a return on investment. There must be belief and a 'can do attitude', to find a way to solve problems and deliver value, to motivate and develop structures that support achievement.

4 Entrepreneur Needs

1. Confidence that their attitude, knowledge and skills are entrepreneurial
2. Understanding business management, leverage and scale.
3. Overcoming industry and government regulatory obstacles
4. Ability to recognise income streams, raise finance and protect rewards

To influence entrepreneur development and entrepreneur thinking, these 4 needs require emphasis and exposure in education and through nurturing and mentoring.

Born or Made Again!

For those supporters who believe entrepreneurs are born and cannot be made in the classroom we must answer 2 questions:

1. Are we teaching the right skills in the right way?
2. What do we need to change, include or dismiss?

The answers to these questions can help design entrepreneur cultures that support entrepreneur development.

One salient point is the recurring theme of chaos in start-up. An entrepreneur environment is of high growth, high activity and high entrepreneur action. However, the support structures are a static efficiency that must assist entrepreneur action and growth, therefore the support structures needed is loose structures with less regulation.

Summary

How all this fits together. Simply put, entrepreneurship has many complexities, however, an in-depth analysis demonstrates certain processes that can help build entrepreneur thinking. When we start to examine the processes of entrepreneurship, we start to accumulate knowledge of the foundations and how entrepreneurs are built. This enables the identification of the ingredients or the building blocks of entrepreneurs and points researchers in the direction of developing strategies that support and promote the attitudes, knowledge and skills of the entrepreneur. Thus, if we can develop entrepreneurial attitude, knowledge and skills we can influence economic stimulation, we can drive economies, create new products and services as well as jobs and other social benefits.

Conclusion

So, through my research I found there are certain skills that entrepreneurs develop, and these are well documented over hundreds of year's writings, we just need to explore and define ways to exploit our knowledge and skills. The key skills of entrepreneurship are coordinating, inventing, leading and managing. These skills help entrepreneurs to pull together all the resources of entrepreneurship including spotting the opportunity, providing a solution, creating a vision to move people toward the results and to manage the rewards from the venture in a positive and creative way to drive more growth and ensure survival. I reality, the entrepreneur has an eye for constant improvement and by improving a current state, old ways are discarded in favour of new and better more effective means of providing pleasure through solutions. This is entrepreneur spirit, a different way of thinking that is the skill of an entrepreneur. Skills can be identified, learned, honed, perfected and replicated.

Entrepreneur skills are important to nations because economic stimulation can be influenced through new ideas and entrepreneur action. Having an entrepreneur mind-set means 'there is always a better way' and this drive will provide new products and services and improve people's lives while also making a profit for the entrepreneur and providing social benefits such as jobs and taxes. Entrepreneurs have a mindset for entrepreneur activity and by encouraging an entrepreneur mindset in young people we are able to influence future entrepreneur decisions and entrepreneur action. Therefore, deciphering and understanding the entrepreneur process is important for the development and promotion of entrepreneurship. The research suggests the focus must be on, 'what do entrepreneurs do', and therefore, the skills of an entrepreneur. Entrepreneurs are found to understand and master the discovery of ideas, exploit the opportunity to achieve results through leadership and manage the value derived from the venture. All four of these can be taught. The probability of entrepreneurship can be increased by showing people how they need to think, act and behave to find constraints, solve a problem, provide solutions, start a business, leverage resources and protect the venture rewards for economic benefit.

Entrepreneurs need up to date and relevant business, industry, regulatory and compliance information in order to compete for market share. Therefore, education plays a vital role in developing entrepreneurs and a future workforce. However, schools and universities turn out many students but many of whom will be thinking of employment rather than a career in entrepreneurship. Even business students are likely to have their sights set on employment or a better job because they have a business degree or an MBA. Is this because we think entrepreneurship is about sales, marketing, strategy, finance and HR instead of entrepreneur culture, mind-set, spirit, leap and entrepreneur structures? There seems to be a 'group think' phenomenon underlying and fettering the development of career entrepreneurs in favour of a bias toward making young people ready for employment. Arguably, this is because of the theory that entrepreneurship is more suited to a 'special person' and our education systems are unable to facilitate the countries need for entrepreneur action. The other argument is that educational systems breed the entrepreneur out of students instead of nurturing young people to choose between employment and entrepreneurship. Thus, the current education system fails potential entrepreneurs meaning young potential entrepreneurs must be prepared to find their own way to learn or fail their dreams, or the system fails them!

Arguably, entrepreneur skills are basic human instincts and when encouraged and rewarded entrepreneur ventures are more possible and success more probable. I found that small measures may have a big effect on developing entrepreneur's natural human instincts since there is currently an imbalance in enterprise training for young people in favour of a focus on employment. Therefore, a small shift in educational thinking to accommodate entrepreneur training instead of focus on the 'special person' can have a big influence on future entrepreneur decisions. Then the entrepreneur career option must be an equal choice that may be perceived by some as better and fairer than working for others despite the risk. This also means improving entrepreneur support and reducing barriers so new entrepreneurs have greater probability of success. But creating an entrepreneur culture is dependent upon a different and new way of thinking where entrepreneurship is encouraged alongside traditional employment and start-up barriers are reduced as low as possible with similar access to start-up loans for young people similar to student loans as what makes a difference to venture creation is start-up capital. A great idea, motivation and the competencies to find a way are all meaningless without the money to start. I think, at the very least education systems should explain both career opportunities to include employment and entrepreneurship. However, I accept an attitude to risk is a personal decision at a specific time taking into account rational factors that are procedural and emotional factors that can't be taught in a classroom or gym.

However, we must separate rational and emotional from entrepreneur training. We are able to explain the factors of uncertainty and the risks that may be presented as a result of the uncertainty. This means contingencies may be put in place to mitigate the risk to an acceptable level and if not, we can make a decision on whether the likely benefits outweigh the potential risks. So, while not advocating entrepreneurs should be risk averse or risk takers it is possible to demonstrate that an understanding of risk management can be taught in a classroom. If we don't start to understand entrepreneurship in new and better ways, we are depriving future generations of a vital economic resource and may be unconsciously bounding entrepreneurs from starting their own businesses but also from contributing in a more focused manner if employment is preferred.

Entrepreneurship is clearly a special set of skills but mostly it requires entrepreneur system thinking. Developing entrepreneur skills means including entrepreneur processes in our daily lives so we begin to naturally examine our environment for entrepreneur opportunities that may be grasped today, tomorrow or passed on to others such as entrepreneurial teams or where the idea is an intrapreneurial one to employers. Enhancing special skills can be achieved through positive interpretation of life events and experiences and this must be encouraged to nurture the 4 key entrepreneur skills.

1. Coordinators who pull together all the necessary resources
2. Inventors, discovering ideas, innovation, adaptation and improvisation
3. Leaders, motivate and achieve results
4. Managers, measure and consider risks and build networks

We can see that Lord Bilimoria's statement unfolds with dramatic insight when we analyse entrepreneurs in this simple way and focus on the tasks that entrepreneurs actually do.

'Entrepreneurs have an idea,
Want to take it somewhere and
Against all the odds making it happen!'

In most cases an entrepreneur learns these skills to survive through work or life experience that may or may not include education. This may be a more difficult means of learning a craft compared with traditional practical vocations where teaching and assessment is mapped out for the progression of the professions such as law or accounting and vocations such as carpentry or computer programming. However, it is beneficial that entrepreneurship is open to all people as every trade or profession offers opportunity to develop scalable businesses from top accounting and law firms, airlines, manufacturing, retailing, search engines, social media apps, and taxi companies or driverless cars. There are no boundaries beyond the limiting beliefs we impose on ourselves. However, parents, families, friends, media and institutions that hold narrow views about an entrepreneur being a special person will hold back every potential entrepreneur unless they believe they can do it. We must think differently.

Entrepreneurs need instruction in how to recognise opportunity, find ideas, achieve results or manage value. We need to think differently in many ways, not just entrepreneur thinking but how we train and develop our young people. The Internet is changing the world every minute of every day. The speed of change is unprecedented, technology gaps and amazing technological advances create opportunities on a global scale. Anyone with a computer and internet access can exploit an opportunity in a global market instantly, opportunity is huge, and this is an entrepreneur's playground. Young people need help to acquire an entrepreneur mindset as in other countries such as USA or India where entrepreneurship is encouraged and ubiquitous. The development of entrepreneur skills is a double-edged sword since it raises the opportunity of venture creation and the skills of the entrepreneurial workforce. This can provide inimitable competitive advantage and contribute to businesses and the economy in as yet unperceived entrepreneurial ways as the speed of change is tamed and exploitable.

Through examining what entrepreneurs do we can identify the process and the key skills that may be passed on. Simply put entrepreneur definitions focus on inventing, leading and managing. Therefore, key skills should focus on the discovery of ideas, achieving results and managing the venture value. These key skills should be wrapped around our normal education systems. This will provide a habitual grounding in practical entrepreneur skills unleashing an ambition of potential entrepreneurs. It is with interest that we have observed entrepreneurs give up a business to go to college, other entrepreneurs who want to work in a business and the many employees who want to be entrepreneurs! Is it a case of the grass is greener?

Having the skills is a wonderful start and leaping into entrepreneur action, well that's a personal decision! And, money, value, experience and know-how, well, entrepreneurs are either born with this type of capital or they make their own. But young people can benefit from a choice of 'student loan' or 'start up loan' and this type of shift could be revolutionary to kick-start entrepreneur ventures. Investment in young people that promotes debt and hopelessness and destroys dreams of fantastic jobs or entrepreneurship is hardly a great economic initiative and unfortunately, it has become a norm for a desperate generation of young people who are ill-informed about the perils of debt-ridden university outcomes and are deprived of essential entrepreneur skills that may make a difference.

A natural human instinct is to be free so it's no surprise that independence is often on a list of entrepreneurial traits and where would an entrepreneur be if they weren't optimistic, and optimism is everywhere too? Similarly, the need for achievement is not only found in an entrepreneurial type of person. For every advocate that entrepreneurs are born there are equally a number who argue entrepreneurs are made. The debate rages on but it is possible to find all the traits of an entrepreneur in ordinary people. That's because ordinary people have some entrepreneur skills but perhaps not sufficient skills, ability and confidence in entrepreneurship and business to launch an entrepreneurial venture.

One approach is to consider everyone as having entrepreneurial capital and this varies depending on exposure to life events, personality and definition fit. We can train ourselves to be more business savvy, expose ourselves to different experiences and learn to interpret things in different ways (even past events that may one thing to us may in fact be interpreted in a different light!). This may increase the value of a person's entrepreneurial capital, but it takes entrepreneur action to become an entrepreneur.

Entrepreneurs balance their own personal values with the company vision. When these align, we have a formula for success. However, entrepreneur action requires creativity in producing solutions and designing procedures to achieve objectives and to manage value and that includes risk management.

While freedom is a natural human characteristic, so is survival, people will fight for survival, to protect their family, friends, colleagues and countryman etc. and in our fight for freedom and survival there must be self-confidence and self-belief or we fail before we start, the same applies to entrepreneurship. In countries such as India and Africa where survival is a daily fight entrepreneurship is prevalent! However, in countries like the UK, Spain or France entrepreneurship is seen by many to be of lower importance as the state infrastructure creates an environment for businesses to prosper, businesses create jobs and employees are trained through schools, colleges and universities.

Business management takes many hours of hard work, a positive attitude to learn from mistakes, an understanding that you control what happens, an enthusiastic and determined attitude. Great support also helps but self-mentoring, analysis and modeling, asking questions and feeding your brain with new information can also help to support progress, this type of self-analysis may be more natural to some than others, but everyone can learn to self-critique. The more we understand our actions within the existing environment then the better our constructive criticism and the decisions and actions we can take to survive entrepreneurship.

Finally, with 600m young people unemployed would a nation be better placed to invest in entrepreneurial ventures than training students to work for employers when there is little hope of finding employment in a depleted labour market? We can find new ways to develop entrepreneurs, increase the likelihood of opportunity recognition, improve the attractiveness of the entrepreneur leap, and increase the probability of venture success and survival.

We can start with identifying the process of entrepreneurship and the nurturing of this vital human characteristic for the benefit of all mankind. Hopefully, this short text will help people think like entrepreneurs, develop an entrepreneurial mind-set and a can-do attitude. This will help potential entrepreneurs focus on the right things and contribute to economic activity as an entrepreneur or intrapreneur.

The Four Entrepreneur Secrets (Reviewed)

ORGANISE - Coordinator, Identify Value

Opportunity Recognition
Resources
Growth
Achievement
Niche or Not
Improvise
Stress-tolerance
Exploitation

GROWTH - Inventor, Create Value

Goals
Reality
Options
Who Will Win When
Tracking
Help

PAIDBACK - Leader, Deliver Value

Planning
Action
Interest, Ingenuity, Intention
Desire
Benefits
Advantages
Connection
Knowledge

PROTECT - Manager, Manage Value

Process
Risk, Reporting and Relations
Operations
Tactics
Employees
Capital (not just cash)
Time

The Entrepreneur Driver is CASH – Financial Capital

Capital
Assessment
Streams
Hedge

Recommendations

My recommendations focus on how to move entrepreneurship forward. We can move entrepreneurship forward with focus on the areas that matter most. However, the primary focus must be to create an environment of inclusive entrepreneurship. Arguably, best achieved through focus on developing training and education initiatives that encourage entrepreneur thinking at a grass roots cultural level. Focus on the Four Entrepreneur Secrets, The Entrepreneur Driver, The Four Barriers to Entrepreneurship, The 7 Reasons for the Entrepreneur Barriers and The Two Type of Entrepreneur and Motivations.

Entrepreneur Culture

Entrepreneurs are nurtured and encouraged, and this must start from an early age to demonstrate that ordinary people can be Captains of industry. Schools, colleges and university can play a big part too and if we want to change the culture of the nation to be more supportive of entrepreneurship then start at grass roots level. The education and skills courses do not turn out entrepreneurs and while entrepreneur training is difficult because of the uniqueness of entrepreneurs, products and the environments the basic entrepreneur skills are replicable. However, it's highly likely that our universities do not really relate to entrepreneurship and should be reviewed to be more practical. Education should focus on developing the skills of an entrepreneur before teaching about running a business. Business is not entrepreneurship, there are many self-employed businesspeople running businesses, but entrepreneurs are focused on scale. This is a big difference.

Entrepreneur Mindset

A can do attitude stems from thinking about things in a different way. Developing and entrepreneur mindset is fundamental to increasing entrepreneur activity and learning about entrepreneur skills is fundamental to entrepreneur spirit. Students seem to enjoy rhetorical speeches from real entrepreneurs with an entrepreneur mindset. Mentors. Why is it so difficult to grasp entrepreneurship except from people who have done it? Do we allow the economic future of our children rest with unstructured and ad hoc teachings? Is this the only way? Education is still failing children who need education in how to run a business (and the skills of entrepreneurship) and we do little to attempt to bottle the "Mentors entrepreneur talents'.

Entrepreneur Spirit

Entrepreneur spirit is to actively seek out change rather than waiting for it to happen and to embrace the process we must learn to ask what is wrong with the current state of affairs and how can we do it better? By developing a process that is change seeking we can influence the speed of economic development.

Entrepreneur Leap

Why don't more latent entrepreneurs make the entrepreneurial leap? Is it money, skills or referents or a coming together of all 3? Is it opportunity recognition?

It's difficult to influence the motivation to take a risk. However, we can build confidence, develop entrepreneur skills and improve the chance of opportunity recognition. Startups need access to finance however the report finds existing financial support is also failing entrepreneurs. However, an Australian report suggests the barrier to the entrepreneur leap is more about a lack of ideas than a lack of funding.

Entrepreneur Structures

Reduce the structures that fetter entrepreneurs and new businesses. Entrepreneurs are free thinkers, achievers and economic contributors. They are first innovators, adaptors and improvisers and these dynamics require loose structures. Secondly, entrepreneurs are motivators who move themselves, individuals, teams, suppliers, customers and suppliers toward some common goals that require low, medium and high structure as appropriate. Finally, an entrepreneur's success mostly relies on credibility and reputation, which eventually require high management structures. Thus, entrepreneur ventures should be seen as economic contributors providing economic advantages such as jobs and other social benefits and so low structures must be considered on start-up such as relaxed state obligations and zero taxation whereas mature organisations may be more highly structured with higher survival rates and high government structures.

Entrepreneur Diversity (Change and Groupthink)

Mentors must focus on venture survival as well as growth. Most businesses fail because the idea did not serve a want or a need and without a gap in the market there is no market for the product or service. So mentoring help must include:

1. Ensure new ventures identify and test the market need.
2. Financial planning must be robustly executed.
3. The business values and all stakeholders must be aligned.
4. There must be inimitable competitive advantage, don't compete on price.
5. Ensure selling price accounts for all costs and provides value for money.

Change the idea or create a market but don't dampen the inspiration of future entrepreneurs. Entrepreneurship can grow by finding new solutions to the same old problems that result from the group think phenomenon amongst those who support entrepreneurs. Entrepreneur support is dogged with a reluctance to change and reach out to the masses of entrepreneurs and provide the support that is really required. Mentoring is failing entrepreneurs because the support is ad hoc and regulatory invasive in many cases, entrepreneurship is not about bureaucracy it's about scalable growth, income streams and sales.

Entrepreneur Roles

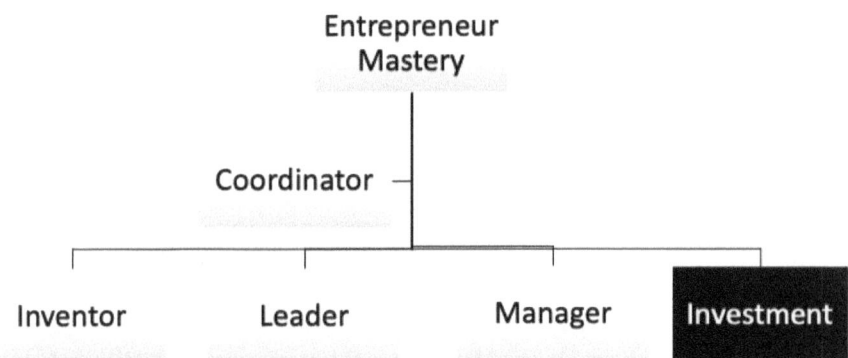

Types of Capital

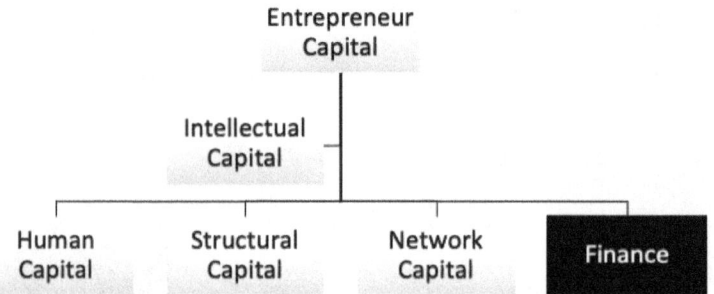

Entrepreneur Support & Entrepreneur Capital

Entrepreneurs can benefit from focus on the ingredients of entrepreneurship and by demanding more from the support available to them. Existing support must be challenged by entrepreneurs and improved by the suppliers; this must be a natural conclusion based on the failings of existing structures. Entrepreneur support should focus on developing and measuring the 5 types of Entrepreneur Capital (Capital meaning value and not just cash).

Entrepreneur Capital – the value of an entrepreneurs experience and skills
Developing entrepreneur capital through dedicated and structured entrepreneur training and through exposure to life events and experiences.

Human Capital – the unwritten and under-utilised ideas and know-how
Focus on human capital through training young people and potential or latent entrepreneurs in the skill of innovation. It is essential to identify constraints and generate a steady flow of ideas that help develop practical and workable solutions that entrepreneurs can exploit for profit.

Structural Capital – Everything left in the building when the gates are locked
Designing structural capital to leverage resources and scale the business. Entrepreneurs must quickly develop income streams and find ways to drive cash-flow through the business so that funds can be re-invested for growth.

Network Capital – All the relations that make the business tick!
Understanding how reputation is key to building Network Capital and why relationships are our most valuable asset. Develop training programmes that focus on Network Capital.

Financial Capital – Any cash, money, investment, loans or finance etc.
Financial Capital should not focus on direct cash implications such as start-up funds, loans or Angel investors but we should also focus on indirect assistance through the Zero rating of taxation for new ventures for 12 months to 60 months for turnover under £100,000. This will help businesses survive the toughest first years and ensure long-term success and jobs for the future positive effects on the economy. Think more long-term.

Quote: "Use the Difficulty"

Michael Caine

101 Tips

1. Generate sales action with a conscious focus on brand impact.
2. Keep debt low with aggressive strategies.
3. Manage cash flow as this is the lifeblood of the business, adopt aggressive cash retention strategies.
4. Invest in scale for growth and hard work for success. Triple your growth by doubling your knowledge and self-development.
5. Manage people properly or you will lose, and they will leave. Create a high performing environment where through hard work people achieve their objectives and thereby you achieve yours.
6. Hire right and we all win. Best people for best jobs make us the best.
7. Brief and de-brief staff to learn from mistakes and improve our offer and value. Be fearless of change in favour of opportunity tomorrow.
8. Keep it simple stupid KISS
9. Sustainable growth is achievable, fast growth is more difficult.
10. Spread growth activities as there are always winners and losers. Winning formulas become exhausted, new formulas ensure new growth.
11. Contingency plans are the best laid plans. Think, plan and execute a brilliant idea correctly, first time.
12. Know your market and practice to deliver value and serve your customers well. It's not genius!
13. Watch the competition or they will steal your market and the food from your mouths, their jealousy is your best accolade!
14. Take action and inspire others to do the same. We have to ASK for the business, or nothing happens!
15. Say what you mean and follow it through, encourage integrity and perfection in yourself and others. Only the best is good enough.
16. List the things you find acceptable and those that are unacceptable, these are the standards you are willing to live by, make every effort to live by your highest standards.
17. Create your vision, know why you want to achieve and deliver the vision and what you have to do each day and then do it, constantly and convincingly even in the light of heavy criticism. Be iconic!
18. The devils in the detail, make the complicated simple not simpler.
19. Aim to connect with people, customers, clients and suppliers to reach win / win outcomes (no matter how big or small), we want to do business over and over again.
20. Become an expert. know your subject, research the best people in your field, model their behaviour and learn from their successes and failures.
21. Ask great questions to receive considered answers and reach better conclusions that make more certain decision making! Failure can mean success if you question hard enough.
22. Ignore logic. Focus on what works, don't try to re-invent the wheel but continue to solve problems through innovation, adaptation and improvisation. The best solutions are often the simplest but deliver value

and reduce cost.

23. Be kind and generous, especially with your time and undivided attention but don't be a pushover!

23. Focus on network expansion and you will never be isolated.

25. FEAR: False Expectations Appearing Real

26. Remember, we always have a choice. A job well done feels better than a job half done.

27. Two ears and one mouth, use them proportionally and when you speak, say it confidently and concisely, don't waffle.

28. We only get one opportunity to create a great first impression.

29. We are continuously negotiating, always think of a BATNA, your best alternative to a negotiated agreement!

30. In discussions tailor your message toward the things your customer associates with this will help them focus on the positive message such as value and dilute the negative parts of the discussion such as payment.

31. Say what you mean and deliver on your handshake, don't let people down, you will never be forgiven.

32. Make difficult discussions a priority, build your confidence to open doors and ease relations.

33. Quality of life and longevity is our ultimate long-term goal, we need our health to enjoy our autumn years, our short term goals must be to guard against ill health and accidents and maintain mental focus, physical energy and inspiration.

34. Be slow to hire and fast to fire, people mistakes can be costly, great new hires bring new impetus.

35. Don't procrastinate but remember the path to hell is paved with good intentions so get things done, fast! Make a good start and a great finish.

36. Pressure is self-induced and we bring this on ourselves when we do not have enough time to complete a task to our set standards. Give yourself more time.

37. We are remembered for our contributions; how can we contribute to the lives of others.

38. Strengths are great, and weaknesses are opportunities to improve.

39. Focus, we can achieve what we focus on.

40. Do things to make others appreciate your efforts, contribute. donate your life to a cause larger than yourself and transform the world.

41. Focus on cash flow management, money come money go! Know about every penny.

42. Be confident about your product or service.

43. Focus on one customer at a time and 'Ask' them to buy your products or services.

44. Have a strategy to self-promote, don't leave it to chance.

45. Act on your self-promotion strategy.

46. Equilibrium is death, so change with market, customers, technology

etc. to favour the status quo means no progress, and comfortable becomes uncomfortable.

47. Reinvent, adapt, engineer, remap, reposition, whatever it takes to stay ahead of the pack.

48. Dedicate time for customer, client, partner and employee communication through social media.

49. Be a master at being different from your competitors.

50. Aim to make your customers raving fans! Think differently leave them exasperated, fulfilled and wanting. Start with turning angry customers into opportunity.

51. We have to speculate to accumulate but don't be frivolous.

52. Find ways to increase customer contact, be credible, trustworthy and 'be there' 24/7.

53. The business culture must reflect success.

54. Be organised, everything has a place and everything in its place.

55. Ensure you take your holiday breaks and so do your employees.

56. Focus on building broad and strong social, customer, supplier and business relationships.

57. Learn to self-mentor and try to grow every day.

58. Find a mentor who is happy to help you grow too.

59. Focus on your original vision, trust it, hang it on your wall, include it in your life and refer to it regularly. Don't focus on vision doubters.

60. We can accomplish great things in 5 years, 10 years and 20 years, write down what you would like to achieve. Push others to achieve more.

61. Sell your products at the best price! Research your market and get the balance right to ensure supply, sales and profits.

62. Ensure we offer additional and related products to each customer.

63. Build systems to get leverage and time off!

64. Deal with hard tasks early in the day when you are at your best.

65. Hire specialists to do the business enhancing tasks to the highest standard, leaving you to focus on what you do best.

66. Focus on GROWTH and be an expert on your market.

67. Measure everything. If it can be measured it can be improved.

68. Have work life balance (this is not time management).

69. Have fun, be happy.

70. Write a blog or keep a diary, a person who knows their weaknesses also knows their strengths.

71. Workout, exercise helps us stay healthy.

72. Eat well and healthily.

73. Start your day early.

74. Go to bed early and sleep well.

75. Leave time for reading something that interests you.

76. Just as in work a process leverages results, your daily routine will maximise your performance.

77. Leave time for yourself, even if it's a 15 minute uninterrupted walk.

78. You only have one chance to create a great first impression, make it.
79. Become an expert in your field. Be the best in the world.
80. Be with people you want to do business with.
81. Develop, improve and invest in your-self.
82. Improve your negotiation skills and have a BATNA!
83. Be active in your community, forums, charity, social events.
84. Delegate, conditionally and unconditionally.
85. Be open to learning, think how we can apply things we have learned to our business, our industry and our people.
86. We never fail when we learn from mistakes.
86. Look for constraints and think about innovation.
87. Choose to be always motivated.
88. Some people get it, some people can be helped to get it, some never get it!
89. Rules: bend them, break them, write them and rewrite them!
90. Resourcefulness is a measure of effectiveness and to be effective we must first be resourceful!
91. Right place, right time, always, location, location, location.
92. Optimism is a door to opportunity.
93. Relationships, trust and reputation equal more relationships, more trust and greater credibility.
94. Network, network, network.
95. Master intangibles.
96. Keep amazing records and know how you got there! This builds Goodwill!
97. Build your business around your life, not your life around your business.
98. Be positive about criticism, there's no smoke without fire.
99. Complacency is a disease. So is procrastination.
100. Happiness is an emotion; a state of mind and money doesn't buy it.
101. Entrepreneurship is not about tax or company registration or regulations etc, it's about relations, providing value and getting results.

About The Author

I was a retail manager, managing a 26,000 square feet department store without any business qualifications. My training had been in house and focused on taking things apart and rebuilding them. We would look at a problem and ask, 'where are we now, what's wrong with our current situation?' We would compare ourselves against the best and say that's where we want to be. Then work out how we would get there, how we can move from a place of dissatisfaction to a more favourable place? A Harvard MBA Entrepreneur headed our £130m business. I wanted to get some business knowledge and find out all about entrepreneurship.

I have been quite surprised how broad a subject entrepreneurship is, I looked at leadership and management, economics, psychology, psychiatry, sociology and business gurus, mentors and coaches as well as entrepreneurs and the secrets of selling. It's been a fascinating insight into the most important but little understood phenomenon of entrepreneurship.

"I would say our understanding of entrepreneurship, as a subject is now where flight was at the start of the 20th Century".

We have lots more to learn. Particularly since university business schools are very poor at turning out entrepreneurs and despite government support being available entrepreneur ventures have a very high rate of failure. Is it the lack of ideas, the lack of funding or our lack of understanding of entrepreneurship as a subject that leads to failure? Whatever the reason it's time for change as we simply cannot leave the most important economic activities to chance, struggling start-ups, unstructured support or look back at another decade of high failure rates.

So, over the next ten years I studied entrepreneurs, sales, business and administration, project management and health and safety and researched the business rhetoric on the world wide web. Then I spent time with intellectual capital accountants who measure both tangible and intangible assets or non-financial assets and held a position as a managing director. My research paper about entrepreneurs working inside organisations was published in a training journal by Emerald in 2011. Then I reached a point where I thought that if only entrepreneurship was a product, how would an entrepreneur achieve leverage? I felt I had a message to share. This has become Entrepreneur Thinking. My previous work is available on Amazon Books.

References

Adams, J.S. (1965). Injustice in Social Exchange. In L. Berkowitz (Ed). Advances in Experimental Social Psychology. Vol 2. New York: Academic Press.

Aernoudt, Rudy. 2004. Incubators: Tools for Entrepreneurship? Small Business Economics. Vol 23.

Aldrich, H.E. Martinez, M.A. (2001). Many Are Called But Few Are Chosen, An Evolutionary Perspective for the Study of Entrepreneurship. Entrepreneurship Theory & Practice. 25 (4).

Alessandro, A.J. O'Connor, M.J. The Platinum Rule: Discover the Four Basic Business Personalities – and How They Can Lead You To Success. New York Warner Books 1996.

Allport, G.W. 1973. Personality A Psychological Interpretation. New York Jolt. Rinehart & Winston.

Argandona, A. 2001. Corruption: The Corporate Perspective. 2001. Business Ethics: A European Review.Vol 10, 2.

Argyris, C. Schon, D.A. (1978). Organisational Learning: A Theory of Action Perspective. Reading: Addison-Wesley Publishing.

Baker, T. Miner, A. Eesley, D.T. Fake It Until You Make It: Improvisation And New Ventures. Obtained from the internet at http://www.babson.edu/entrep/fer/Babson2001

Baker,T. Miner, A. Eesley, D. (2003). Improvising Firms: Bricolage, Account Giving and Improvisational Competency in the Founding Process. Research Policy, 32

Bansler, J.P. Havn, E.C. Improvisation in Information Systems Development. Information Systems Research. Relevant Theory and Informed Practice, Proceedings of IFIP TC8/WGB.2, July 2004.

Bateman, T.S. Crant, J.M. (1993). The Pro-active Component of Organisational behaviour. A Measure and Correlates. Journal of Organisational behaviour. 14.

Begley, T.M. (1995). 'Using Founder Status, Age of Firm,and Company Growth Rate as the Basis for Distinguishing Entrepreneurs from Managers of Smaller Businesses'. Journal of Business Venturing, 10.

Begley, T.M. Boyd. D.P. (1986). The Relationship of the Jenkins Activity Survey to Type A Behaviour and Business Executives.

Begley, T.M. Boyd. D.P. (1987). 'Psychological Characteristics Associated with Performance in Entrepreneurial Firms and Smaller Businesses'. Journal of Business Venturing. 2.

Birch, D.L. (1979) The Job Creation Process. Unpublished Report, MIT Program on Neighbourhood and Regional Change. Prepared for the Economic Development Administration, United States Department of Commerce, Washington D.C.

Bird. B. (1988). Implementing Entrepreneurial Ideas: The case for intention. Academy of Management Review.

Blaug, M. The Empirical Status of Human Capital Theory: A Slightly Jaundiced Survey. Journal of Economic Literature, 1976.

Block, Z. MacMillan I.C. (1973). Corporate Venturing: Creating New Business Within the Firm. Boston. Harvard Business review Press.

Bolton, B & Thompson, J. (2004). Entrepreneurs. Talent, Temperament, Technique. 2nd Edition. Elsevier.

Bouchard, V. Corporate Entrepreneurship: Lessons from the Field, Blind Spots and Beyond... (2002). EM Lyon European Entrepreneurial Learning, Cahiers De Recherche ISSN: 0183-259X

Boyd, D.P. (1984) Type A behaviour, Financial Performance and Organisational Growth in Small Business Firms. Journal Of Occupational Psychology.

Brazeal, D.V. Herbert, T.T. (1999). The Genesis of Entrepreneurship. Entrepreneurial Theory and Practice.

Breedon, R. 2004. Education and Necessity Mold Entrepreneurs. Wall Street Journal – Eastern Edition. Sept2004. Vol 244. Issue 47.

Brixy, U. Kohaut, S. (1999). Employment Growth Determinants in New Firms in Eastern Germany. Small Business Economics. 13.

Brockhaus, R.H. The Psychology of the Entrepreneur. In Kent, Vesper, Sexton (eds) Encyclopaedia of Entrepreneurship (1982) Prentice Hall.

Burgelman, R.A. (1984). Designs For Corporate Entrepreneurship in Established Firms: California Management Review. Vol. 26. No.3.

Burrell, G. Morgan, G. (1979) Sociological Paradigms and Organisational Analysis, Heinemann, London.

Busenitz, L.W. Barney, J.B. (1997). Differences Between Entrepreneurs and Managers in Large Organisations: Biases and Heuristics in Strategic Decision-making'. Journal of Business Venturing,12.

Burgoyne, J. Pedler, M. Boydell, T. (1991). Towards the Learning Company. London: McGraw-Hill.

Business In Wales. March 2005. Western Mail

Bygrave, W.D. (1989). The Entrepreneurship Paradigm (I): A Philosophical Look at Its Research Methodologies. Entrepreneurship Theory and Practice.

Cabral, L. (1995). Sunk Costs, Firm Size and Firm Growth. Journal of Industrial Economics. 43 (2).

Calori, R. (2000). Ordinary Theorists in Mixed Industries. Organisation Studies. Vol,21. No.6.

Carland, J.W. Hoy, F. Boulton, W.R. Carland **J.A.C**. (1984). 'Differentiating Entrepreneurs from Small Business Owners: A Conceptualisation'. Academy of management Review, 9.

Carland, J.W. Hoy, F. Carland **J.A.C**. (1988). 'Who is an Entrepreneur? Is a Question Worth Asking' American Journal of Small Business. 12.

Caspi, A. & Bem, D.J. (1992). Personality Continuity and Change Across the Life Course. In Review of Personality Social Psychology. Beverley Hills: Sage Publications.

Casson, M.C. (1995). Entrepreneurship and Business Culture. Aldershot. UK.

Casson, M.C. Information and Organisation. A New Perspective on the Theory of the Firm. 1997. Oxford. Clarendon Press.

Casson, M.C. (2003). The Entrepreneur. An Economic Theory. Second Edition. Edward Elgar, Cheltenham UK.

Chakrabarti, A.K. (1991). Industry Characteristics Influencing the Technical Output. A Case of Small and Medium-Sized Firms in the US. R&D Management 21 (2).

Chell, E. Haworth, J. Brearley, S. The Entrepreneurial Personality. 1991. Routledge.

Chen, C.C. Greene, P.G. Crick, A. (1998). 'Does Entrepreneurial Self-efficacy Distinguish Entrepreneurs from Managers?'. Journal of Business Venturing, 13.

Christensen, P.S. Madsen,O.O. Peterson, R. (1989). Opportunity Identification: The Contribution of Entrepreneurship to Strategic Management. Denmark: Aarhus University Institute of Management.

Churchill, N.C. Lewis, V.L.(1986). 'Entrepreneurship Research'. In Sexton, D.L. And Similor,R.W. (Eds), The Art and Science of Entrepreneurship, Cambridge, MA: Ballinger.

Clargaux, Paul. - Entrepreneurs: Creativity Follows Knowledge. Independently published.

Clargaux, Paul. - Entrepreneurs: Born Creative, Made Knowledgeable, Driven by Process. Independently published.

Clargo P, Tunstall R, Leading and Developing an Entrepreneurial Workforce: Development or Decline? Emerald Publishing 2010

Clayton, J. Gambill, B. Harned, D. (1999). The Curse of Too Much Capital: Building New Businesses in Large Corporations. The McKinsey Quarterly, Vol, 3.

Collins, C.J. Hanges, P.J. Locke, E.A. (2004). The relationship of Achievement Motivation to Entrepreneurial Behaviour: A Meta-Analysis. Human Performance.

Collinson, E. Quinn, L. (2002). The Impact of Collaboration Between Industry and Academia On SME Growth. Journal of Marketing, 18.

Cooper, A.C. (1985a) The Role of Incubator Organisations in the Founding of Growth Orientated Firms. Journal of Business Venturing, 1985, 75 – 86.

Cooper, A.C. (1986) Entrepreneurship and High Technology. In D.L. Sexton and R.W.

Smilor, (Eds.), The Art and Science of Entrepreneurship. 1986, 153-168. Cambridge, MA. Ballinger.

Cooper, A.C. & Dunkelberg, W.C. (1981). A New Look At Business Entry. Experience of 1805 Entrepreneurs. In K.H. Vesper (Ed), Frontiers of Entrepreneurial Research 1 – 20. Wellesley, MA. Babson College.

Cooper, A.C. & Dunkelberg, W.C. (1987). Entrepreneurial Research: Old Questions, New Answers and Methodological Issues. American Journal of Small Business 1987. 1 (1) 11 – 23.

Cooper, A.C. & Dunkelberg, W.C. Woo, C. Dennis,W. (1990). New Business In America: The Firms and Their Owners. Washington D.C. NFIB Foundation.

Copulsky, W. McNulty, H.W. 1974. Finding and Keeping the Entrepreneur Management Review. 1974.

Cosmas, S.C. (1982). Lifestyles and Consumption Patterns. Journal of Consumer Research. Vol 8.

Coutu, D.L. Creating the Most Frightening Company on Earth. Harvard Business Review, 00178012, Sept 2000 Vol 78 (5).

Cromie, S. Birley, S. (1992). 'Networking by Female Business Owners in Northern Ireland'. Journal of Business Venturing, 7.

Cromie, S. (2000). Assessing Entrepreneurial Inclinations: Some Approaches and Empirical Evidence. European Journal Of Work and Organisational Psychology. 9.

Crossan, M. Lane, H.W. White, R.E. (1999). An Organisational Learning Framework: From Intuition to Institution. Academy of Management Review, vol 24. No.3.

Crossan, M. Cunha, M. Vera, D. Cunha, J. (2005). Time and Organisational Improvisation. Academy of Management Review. Vol. 30.

Davis, L. R&D Investments, Information and Strategy. Technology Analysis & Strategic Management, Vol 13, (3) 2001.

Deamer, I. Earle, L. (2004). Searching for Entrepreneurship. Industrial and Commercial Training. Vol. 36.

Dehler, G.E. Welsh, M.A. Lewis, M.W. 2001. Critical Pedgogy in the 'new paradigm'. Management Learning. 32.

Desai, M. Gompers, P. Lerner, J. 2003. Institutions, Capital Constraints and Entrepreneurial Firm Dynamics: Evidence from Europe. Harvard Working Paper No.03-59. **Http://ssrn.com/abstract=479982**

Dodd, C. Gordon, I.M. Smart, C. 2004. Further Evidence on the Role Of Gender in Financial Performance. Journal of Small Business Management 2004, 42,4.

Drucker, P. (1985). Innovation and Entrepreneurship. London. Heinman.

Duchesneau, D.A. Gartner, W.B. (1990). A Profile of New Venture Success and Failure in Emerging Industry. Journal of Business Venturing. 5.

Durham University Business School, General Enterprising Tendency (GET) Test. Author, Durham, UK, 1988.

Economic Committee, (1986). The Singapore Economy: New Directions. Singapore: Ministry of Trade and Industry.

Erikson, T. Nerdrum, L. New Venture Management Valuation: Assessing Complementary Capacities by Human Capital Theory. Venture Capital 2001, Vol. 3 No.4.

Evans, D. (1987a). Test of Alternative Theories of Firm Growth. Journal of Political Economy. 95. (4).

Evans, D. (1987b). The Relationship Between Firm Growth, Sizeand Age: Estimates for 100 Manufacturing Industries. Journal of Industrial Economics. 35.

Fast, N. (1978). The rise and Fall of Corporate New Venture Divisions. Ann Arbor, UMI Review Press.

Faupel, C.E. Heroin Use and Criminal Careers. Qualitative Sociology 10, 2, Summer 1987.

Feeser, H.R. & Willard, G.E. (1989) Incubators and Performance. A Comparison of High and Low Growth in High Tech Firms. Journal of Business Venturing. 4(6) 429-441.

Feldman, M. Francis, J. Bercovitz, J. (2005). Creating a Cluster While Building a Firm: Entrepreneurs and The Formation of Clusters. Regional Studies. 39.

Fisher, C. Dowling, P.J. (1999). Support for an HR Approach in Austrailia: The Perspective of Senior HR Managers. Asia, Pacific Journal of Human Resources. 37.

Fligstein, N. (1997). Social Skills and Institutional Theory. American Behavioural Scientist, vol 40.No.4.

Friedman, M. (1953). The Methodology of Positive Economics. In Essays in Positive Economics, ed. University of Chicago Press.

Friedman,V.J. (2002). The Individual as Agent of Organisational Learning. California Management Review.Vol,44. No.2.

Fuller, T. Morgan, P. (2001). Small Enterprises as Complex Adaptive Systems: A Methodological Question. Entrepreneurship and Regional Development, 13.

Futures Group 1984. Characterisations of Innovations Introduced on the US Market in 1982. Report Prepared For The US Small Business Administration Office of Advocacy, Washington D.C.

Gartner, W.B. (1989). 'Who is an Entrepreneur? Is the Wrong Question.' American Journal of Small Business, 12.

Gartner, W.B. (1989). Some Suggestions For Research On Entrepreneurial Traits And Characteristics. Entrepreneurship Theory and Practice.

Gatewood, E.J. Shaver, K.G. Gartner, W.B. (1995). A Longitudinal Study of Cognitive Factors Influencing Start-up behaviours and Success at Venture Creation. Journal of Business Venturing. 10.

Geier, J.G. Downey, D.E. Library of Classical Profile Patterns. Performax Systems International. 1979.

Gibb, A. (2002). In Pursuit of a New Enterprise and Entrepreneurship Paradigm for Learning: Creative Destruction, New Values, New Ways of Doing Things and New Combinations of Knowledge. International Journal of Management Reviews. Vol 4.

Goldberg, A. Cohen, G. Fiegenbaum, A. (2003). Reputation Building: Small Business Strategies For Successful Venture Development. Journal of Small Business Management, 41.

Hamel, G. (1999). Bringing Silicon Valley Inside. Harvard Business Review. Vol, 77. No.5.

Hampson, S.E. (1982). The Construction of Personality, 2nd edition. London, Routledge.

Hampson, S.E. (1984).

Hart, P. Oulton, N. (1999). Gibrat, Galton and Job Generation. International Journal of the Economics of Business. 6 (2).

Harvey-Jones, J. (1995). All Together Now. Mandarin, London.

Herron, L. (1990). The Effects of Characteristics of the Entrepreneur on New Venture Performance. Columbia, SC. University of South Carolina Press.

Hiltrop, J.M. (1995). The Changing Psychological Contract. The Human Resource Challenge of the '90's. European Management Journal. 13 (3).

Himieleski, K.M. Corbett, A.C. Improvisation as a Framework for Investigating Entrepreneurial Action. Academy of Management Best Conference Paper 2003.

Hitt, M.A. Ireland, R.D. Camp, S.M. Sexton, D.L. Strategic Entrepreneurship. Creating a New Mindset. 2002. Blackwell Publishing.

Hiskey, J.T. Political Entrepreneurs and Neo-liberal Reform in Mexico: The Salinas Requisa of the Port of Vera Cruz. Latin Americas Politics and Society. 45:2

Hock, L.N. (2002). Profile of the Enterprise 50 Companies and Other SME's in Singapore. Singapore Management Review.

Hood, J.N. Young, J.E. (1993). 'Entrepreneurship's requisite areas of development: a survey of top executives in successful entrepreneurial firms'. Journal of Business Venturing. 8.

Hochschild, A. (1983). The Manager's Heart. Los Angeles. University of California Press.

Jackson, S. Hitt, M.A. DeNisi, A. S. Managing Knowledge for Sustained Competitive Advantage: Designing Strategies for Human Resource Management. San Francisco: Joey Bass, 2003.

Jencks, C. et al. (1972). Inequality: A reassessment of the effect of Family and Schooling in America. New York. Basic Books.

Johnson, B.R. (1990). 'Toward a Multi-dimensional Model of Entrepreneurship: The Case of Achievement Motivation and the Entrepreneur'. Entrepreneurship Theory and Practice. 14.

Johnson, P.S. & Cathcart, D.G. Dec.(1979) The Founders of new manufacturing Firms: A Note On The Size of Their Incubator Plants. The Journal of Industrial Economics, 28,(2), 219 – 224.

Kanter. R.M. North, J. et al. (1990). Engines of Progress: Designing and Running Entrepreneurial Vehicles in Established Companies. Journal of Business Venturing, Vol.5. No.6.

Kanter. R.M. (1992). The Change Masters: Corporate Entrepreneurs at Work. London – Routledge.

Kanter, R.M. The Middle Manager as Innovator. Harvard Business Review. Jul/Aug 2004. Vol 82, Issue 7/8

Kayes, C.D. (2002). Experimental Learning and its Critics: Preserving the role of experience in Management Learning and Education. Academy of Management Learning and Education. Vol. 1.

Kerins, F. Smith, J.K. Smith, R. Opportunity Cost of Capital for Venture Capital Investors and Entrepreneurs. Journal of Financial and Quantitative Analysis. Vol 39. No.2. June 2004.

Kets de Vries, **M.F.R**. (1977) The Entrepreneurial Personality: A Person at the Crossroads. Journal of Management Studies. Feb.

Kickul, J. Gundy, L.K. (2002). Prospecting for Strategic Advantage: The Proactive Entrepreneurial Personality and Small Firm Innovation. Journal of Small Business Management.

Kihlstrom, R.E. Laffont, J. A General Equilibrium Entrepreneurial Theory of the Firm Formation Based on Risk Aversion.

Kirchoff, B.A. (1994). Entrepreneurship and Dynamic Capitalism, The economics of Business Firm Formation and Growth. Westport, CT. Praeger.

Kirzner, I.M. Entrepreneurial Discovery and the Competitive Market Process: An Austrian Approach. Journal of Economic Literature. Vol 35, Mar 1997.

Knight, F. (1921). Risk, Uncertainty and Profit, New York US. Augustus Kelly.

Koh, H.C. (1996). Testing Hypotheses of Entrepreneurial Characteristics. Journal of Managerial Psychology.

Kuhn, T.S. (1962). The Structure of Scientific Revolutions. Chicago. University Press Chicago.

Kuratko, D.F. Hodgetts, R.M. (1995) Entrepreneurship. Fort Worth. TX. Dryden Press.

Kuratko, D.F. Hodgetts, R.M. (1998) Entrepreneurship: A Contemporary Approach. 4th Ed. Dryden Press.

Kuratko, D.F. Hornsby, J.S. Goldsby, M.G. (2004). Sustaining Corporate Entrepreneurship. Entrepreneurship And Innovation.

Lawler, E.E. Drexler, J.A. Entrepreneurship in the Large Corporation: Is It Possible? Management Review 1981.

Lea, J. Tough on Crime, Tough on Civil Liberties. Criminal Justice Policies and Organised Crime. 2004. Cambrian Law Review.

Lee, Don Y. The Effects of Entrepreneurial Personality, Background and Network Activities on Venture Growth. Journal of Management Studies, 38:4 June 2001.

Littunen, H. (2000). Entrepreneurship and the Characteristics of the Entrepreneurial Personality. International Journal of Entrepreneurial Behaviour. 6.

Londoneurs Survey 2004. Business Link for London Research Reports. Obtained from the internet at **www.businesslink4london.com**

Lumpkin, G.T. Dess,G.G. (1996). Clarifying the Entrepreneurial Orientation Construct and Linking it to Performance. Academy of Management Review, Vol 21. No.3.

Marinova, D. Actualising Innovation Effort: The Impact of Market Knowledge Diffusion in a Dynamic System of Competition. Journal of Marketing Vol 68 July 2004.

McClleland, D.C. (1961) The achieving Society. Princeton NJ. Van Nostrand.

McClleland, D.C. Winter, D.G. (1965) Achievement Motivation Can Be Developed. Harvard Business Review.

McGrath, R. (1999). Falling Forward: Real Options Reasoning and Entrepreneurial Failure. Academy of Management Review. Vol, 24. No.1.

McGrath, R.G. MacMillan, I.C. (2000). The Entrepreneurial Mindset. Boston: Harvard Business School.

McGuire, J. (1964). Theories of Business Behaviour. Englewood Cliffs, NJ: Prentice Hall.

McGuire, J.W. (1976). The small Enterprise in Economics and Organisation Theory. Journal of Contemporary Business. 5, (2).

Macrae, N. (1982). Intrapreneurial Now, The Economist. April 17.

MacKenzie, K.D. House, R. (1978). Paradigm Development in the Social Sciences: A Proposed Research Strategy. Academy of Management Review.

MacMillan, L.C. Siegel, R. Narashima, **S.P.N**. (1985) Criteria Used By Venture Capitalists to Evaluate New Performance. Journal of Business Venturing. 5.

Mangelsdorf, M.E. Bianchi, A. (1994). Entrepreneurial Traits by Nationality. Business Source Premier.

Mata, J. (1994). Firm Growth during Infancy. Small Business Economics. 6.

Meredith, G. G. Nelson, R.E. Neck, P.A. (1982) The Practice of Entrepreneurship, Geneva: International Labour Office.

Miller. D. (1983). The Correlates of Entrepreneurship in Three Types of Firms. Management Science, Vol, 29. No.7.

Miner, J.B. (1990). 'Entrepreneurs, High Growth Entrepreneurs, and Managers: Contrasting and Overlapping Motivational Patterns'. Journal of Business Venturing, 5.

Mingers, J.C. (1995) Information and Meaning: Foundations for an Inter-subjective Account. Information Systems Journal. Vol 5.

Mises, L,V. Human Action. New Haven. Yale University Press. 1949.

Molz, R. Entrepreneurial Managers in Large Organisations. Business Horizons, Sept/Oct 1984.

Moorman, C. Miner, A. (1998). Organisational Improvisation and Organisational Memeory. Academy of Management Review. 23.

Moore, W.H. 2001. Department of Political Science. The Florida State University, Talahassee. **whmoore@garnet.acns.fsu.edu**

Morgan, J. HR Practices for High Performance Organisations. Foundation for Sustainable Economic Development Research Paper April 2001.

Naffziger, D.W. Hornsby, J.S. Kuratko, D.F. A Proposed Research Model of Entrepreneurial Motivation. Entrepreneurship Theory and Practice, Spring 1994.

Nonaka. I. (194). A Dynamic Theory of Organisational Knowledge Creation. Organisation Science, Vol.5. No.1.

Now Management Report. Executives On-line. June 2004 Management Services.

Ogbonna, E. Harris, L.C. (2002). Organisational Culture: A Ten Year, Two Phase Study Of Change In The UK Food Retailing Sector. Journal of Management Studies. 39:5

Orlikowski, W. Knowing in Practice: Enacting a Collective Capability in Distributed Organising. Organisation Science. 13.

Pascale, R. 2000. Surfing the Edge of Chaos. Texere Publishing London.

Pearson, C. Chatterjee, S.R. 2001. Differences and Similarities of Entrepreneurial Characteristics in a Diverse Social Setting – Evidence from Australian and Singaporean Managers. Journal of Enterprising Culture. Vol 9, No. 3.

Pervin, L.A. 1990. Handbook of Personality: Theory and Research. New York. The Guildford Press.

Kamoche, K. Pina, M. Campos, R. Organisational Improvisation and Leadership: A Field Study in Two Computer Mediated Settings. Int. Studies of Management and Organisation. 33.

Pinchot, G. III (1985). Intrapreneuring: Why You Don't Have To Leave The Corporation To Become An Entrepreneur. New York. Harper & Row.

Pinchott, G. Pellman, R. (1999). Intrapreneuring in Action. Berret-Koehler, San Francisco.

Porter, Michael, E. (1985). Competitive Advantage, Creating and Sustaining Superior Performance – The Free Press, New York.

Quinn, J.B. Anderson, P. Leveraging Intellect. Academy of Management Executive. Aug 1996. Vol 10, (3).

Rae, D. (1999). The Entrepreneurial Spirit. Blackhall Publishing, Ireland.

Ramaswani, S.N. Influence of Control Systems on Opportunistic behaviours of Salespeople: A Test of Gender Differences. Journal of Personal Selling & Sales Management. Vol 22. No. 3 Summer 2003.

Reynolds, M. (1999). Critical Reflection and Management Education: Rehabilitating Less Hierarchical approaches. Journal of Management Education. 23.

Reynolds, P.D. Carter, N.M. Gartner, W.B. Greene P.G. 2004. The Prevalence of Nascent Entrepreneurs in the United States: Evidence from the Panel Study of Entrepreneurial Dynamics. Small Business Economics. Nov2004, vol 23. Issue 4.

Roberts, N. Radical Change by Entrepreneurial Design. Acquisition review Quarterly 1998.

Robichaud, Yves. McGraw, E. Roger, Alain. Journal of Development Entrepreneurship, 10849467, Aug2001, Vol 6, Issue 2.

Robson, G. Gallagher, C, Daly, M. (1993). "Diversification Strategy and Practicein Small Firms," International Small Business Journal. 11(2).

Rogers, S. Want to be an Instant Entrepreneur? Business On-line: 10.07.2004

Rogoff, E.G. Lee, M. Suh, D. "Who Done It?" Attributions by Entrepreneurs and Experts of the Factors that Cause and Impede Small Business Success. Journal of Small Business Management 2004. 42 (4).

Romanelli, E. Schoonhaven, K. (2001), 'The Local Origins Of New Firms', in K. Choonhave and E. Romanelli (eds), The Entrepreneurial Dynamic. Stanford University Press US.

Rosch, E. (1978). 'Principles of Categorisation', in E. Rosch and B.B. Lloyd (eds) Cognition and Categorization, Hillsdale, N.J: Erlbaum.

Ross, Sandy. 1996. Think "ME, INC." Dec 1996, HRPLD News. **www.sandyross.ca**

Ross, Glenn. 2003. Ethical Beliefs, work problem-solving strategies and learning styles as mediators of tourism marketing entrepreneurialism. Journal of Vacation Marketing. Vol 9. No. 2.

Rousseau, D.M. (1995). Psychological Contracts in Organisations: Understanding Written and Unwritten Agreements. Thousand Oaks: Sage Publications.

Roux Dufort, C. Vidaillet, B. (2003). The difficulties of Improvising in Crisis Situations. Int. Studies of Management and Organisation. 33.

Schere, J.C. (1982) Tolerance of Ambiguity as a Discriminating Variable Between Entrepreneurs and Managers. Academy of Management Proceedings.

Schumpeter, J.A. (1934). The Theory of Economic Development, Cambridge, Mass. Harvard University Press.

Schumpeter, J. (1942). Capitalism, Socialism and Democracy. New York. Harpers & Row.

Schuster, F.E. Morden, L. Baker, T.E. McKay, I.S. Dunning, K.E. & Hagan, C.M. (1997). Management Practice, Organisation Climate and Performance – An Exploratory Study. Journal of Applied Behavioural Science. 33.

Senge, P. (1990a). The Fifth Disciplin. The Art and Practice of the Learning Organisation. New York. Doubleday Currency.

Shapero, A. Sokol, L. (1982). The Social Dimensions of Entrepreneurship in Kent, Sexton & Vesper's (eds) Encyclopaedia of Entrepreneurship. Englewood Cliffs, NJ. Prentice-Hall

Shane, S. (2003). A General Theory of Entrepreneurship. Edward Elgar Publishing.

Shane, S. Kurana, R. (2001). 'Career Experiences and Firm Foundings', paper presented at the Academy of Management Meetings.

Shaver, K.G. Scott, L.R. (1991). 'Person, Process. Choice: The Psychology of New Venture Creation. Entrepreneurship Theory and Practice.

Simon, H.A. (1991). Bounded Rationality and Organisational Learning. Organisation Science, Vol,2.

Smith, S. Marcum, D. New School. TD October 2003.

Stevenson, H.H. Sahlman, W.A. (1989) The Entrepreneurial Process in P.Burns and J Dewhurst (eds) Small Business and Entrepreneurship.

Stormer, F. Kline, T. Goldenberg, S. Measuring Entrepreneurship with the General Enterprising Tendency (GET) Test: Criterion-related Validity and Reliability. Human Systems Management. 18, 1999.

Thompson, M.A. Kahnweiler, W.M. (2002). An Exploratory Investigation of Learning Culture Theory and Employee Participation in Decision Making. Human Resource Development Quarterly. Vol 13.

Tsang, **E.W.K**. (1998). Can *guanxi* [connections] be a Source of Sustained Competitive Advantage for doing Business in China. Academy of Management Executive. 12.

Ucbasaran, D. Westhead, P. Wright, M. Binks, M. (2003). Does Entrepreneurial Experience Influence Opportunity Identification? The Journal of Private Equity.

Venkataraman, S. MacMillan, I.C. McGrath, I.G. (1992). Progress On Research on Corporate Venturing. In K. Sexton, ed., Sdtate of the Art in Entrepreneurship. Boston: PWS-Kent Publishing.

Venkataraman, S. (1997). The distinctive Domain of Entrepreneurship Research. In J Katz, & Brockhaus R. (Ed), Advances in Entrepreneurship, Firm Emergence and Growth: Greenwich: JAI Press.

Vesper. K.H. (1985). A New Direction or Just a New Label? In J. Kao & H. Stevenson, eds., Entrepreneurship: What it is and How to Teach it. Boston. Harvard Business School Press.

Waller, M.J. Conte, J. Gibson, C. Carpenter, M. (2001). The Effect of Individual Perceptions of Deadlines on Team Performance. Academy of Management Review. 26.

Watson, R. Zinkhan, G. Leyland, P. (2004). Object Orientation. A Tool for Enterprise Design. California Management Review. 46.

Weber, R. (1997) Ontological Foundations of Information Systems. Coopers & Lybrand, Melbourne.

Weick, K. (1999). Sensemaking as an Organisational Dimension of Global Change. In J. Dutton and D Cooperrider (eds), The Human Dimensions of Global Change. Sage, Thousand Oaks, CA.

Yin, R.K. (1999). Case Study Research Design and Methods. 3rd Edition. Sage Publications London.

Yoffie, D.B. Bergenstein, S. Creating Political Advantage: The Rise of the Corporate Political Entrepreneur. California Management Review. Vol 28, 1, 1985.

Zahra, S.A. (1993). A Conceptual Model of Entrepreneurship as Firm behaviour: A Critique and Extension. Entrepreneurship Theory and Practice, Vol, 17. No.4.

Zarha, S.A. (1991). Predictors and Financial Outcomes of Corporate Entrepreneurship: An Exploratory Study. Journal of Business Venturing. Vol 6.

"Happy Beautiful Day"

Ian Phillips

Entrepreneur Thinking

Entrepreneur Thinking is a route to developing intraprenurs in your organisation. Over 300 years of research, entrepreneur definitions, modern theories and a new multi-disciplinary approach finds that people have entrepreneur value. Entrepreneurs are considered the single most important economic factor in driving economic growth and providing social benefits like jobs and paying taxes, therefore, we need to know much more about how entrepreneurs do what they do, how they think! Most research into entrepreneurs takes a narrow approach focusing only on successful entrepreneurs. This means many areas of entrepreneur activity remain uncovered, until now. Broaden your view of entrepreneurs by examining entrepreneurs as if they were a product and if so, what would an entrepreneur do with entrepreneurship? They wouldn't be limited by the born or made argument, that's a fact. Entrepreneurs are unbounded! This is a completely new way of developing people inside of organisations, it's entrepreneur thinking.

'We are born with zero entrepreneur capital; we build entrepreneur capital as we travel through our life or business experiences and the journey is more fruitful when we know the 4 secrets of entrepreneurs and make an entrepreneur leap!

If you ever wondered what entrepreneurs do and how they do it in a practical sense so that we can develop individual intrapreneurs within an organisational entrepreneur culture, then this is the book for you. Entrepreneur Thinking helps you unlock the 4 secrets of entrepreneurship and demonstrates how your people can think like entrepreneurs. If you are wondering what entrepreneurs do, are thinking of starting a business, want employees to be intrapreneurs, then this is a great place to start. The 4 entrepreneur secrets are very significant for mature businesses who want to improve intrapreneur performance or who are interested in modern motivational change management techniques. Ultimately, Entrepreneur Thinking must be on the desk of every entrepreneur, potential entrepreneur, latent entrepreneur, intrapreneur, business manager and anyone who wants to make a difference.

Entrepreneur Thinking identifies the 4 secrets of entrepreneurship and demonstrates how to recognise opportunity, improve the possibility of entrepreneur action, increase the probability of success and venture survival. Identifying the secrets of entrepreneurship means that anyone can be their own entrepreneur mentor and access the tools and models that will really help you succeed.

The benefit of Entrepreneur Thinking is academic theory converted to practical business models and manageable checklists. Readers will be able to identify how entrepreneurs spot opportunity, provide solutions, make things happen and protect the venture rewards, sometimes against all the odds.

Entrepreneur Thinking is the MBA in Entrepreneurship that will help develop intrapreneurs and drive an entrepreneur culture meaning success in work, business and social life too!